CASES IN
FINANCIAL SERVICES MARKETING

Hooman Estelami
Fordham University

Cover image by Shatterstock.com

Contact the author in care of Bahar Books, 785 Old Kensico Road, White Plains, NY
info@baharbooks.com

Editor: Rosemarie McCormack

First published by Bahar Books,
785 Old Kensico Road, White Plains, NY 10603
http://baharbooks.com

ISBN: 978-1-939099-70-9

This book is printed on acid-free paper.
Printed in the United States of America

TABLE OF CONTENTS

INTRODUCTION

The objective of this case book is to provide practitioners and educators in the field of financial services marketing with a resource to empower learning through application of management concepts. The cases included in this book demonstrate a range of marketing challenges faced by managers in various financial institutions. They provide readers with information necessary to formulate managerial solutions to improve company performance. These cases can be used as basis for discussion in formal classes, specialized workshops, as well as executive training modules. A summary of the various cases is provided below.

Sacramento Financial Group examines a financial institution's desire to grow into new markets. The case profiles the decision to introduce an innovative financial solution into a new consumer marketplace. Readers can use this case to conduct market assessment and project potential product success.

KR-20 profiles a loan application processing service for personal loans. The product featured in this case is examined both in the context of its competitive features and price points. The case enables readers to conduct competitive benchmarking and to examine the price and value proposition of the service.

Farmers Bank of Virginia demonstrates the challenges faced by a community bank in modernizing its services. The case presents readers with both primary and secondary market research results, which can be used to formulate a strategy for reviving the bank's marketing portfolio.

AssetsGuard examines the introduction of innovative insurance services in the context of an identity theft product. The case provides data on underlying risks, market potential, competitive offerings, and costs, and it enables readers to formulate product launch recommendations in the insurance industry.

Liberty Asset Financing is a case focused on credit and financing solutions for commercial markets. The case presents readers with information on asset financing services. Readers can use detailed primary market research information to determine optimal pricing for the service.

Lexzmmar Investments provides an overview of the evolution of an investment management organization with a long history and unique marketing traditions. The case presents readers with market response data in relation to outreach campaigns, and challenges readers to determine an optimal launch strategy for a new investment product being considered by the firm's senior executives.

Tire Insurance Program demonstrates the desire of a regional bank to expand its operations into new markets. Specifically, the case profiles expansion of the product line into the consumer insurance market for automobile tire failures. Test market data are presented and readers can use this data to examine the market potential for this product at various price points.

Georgia Supplemental profiles the geographic growth of a financial institution beyond state borders. Readers can use the case to assess the business impact of expansion into a new market, recognize the challenges facing the distribution process and determine the needed resources for such an expansion.

Phoenix Cards Inc. shows the unique challenges that arise when managing change in the distribution of financial services. The case specifically discusses prepaid gift cards and supplemental insurance products. The case examines the hurdles a financial institution faces when evolving into new service delivery modes.

Home Endorsers Inc. focuses on the mortgage generation business. The case context is that of a mortgage brokerage firm that is faced with competitors whose deceptive marketing actions challenge the firm's own business principles. Readers are provided with focus group summaries and consumer complaint data and asked to formulate an appropriate response strategy.

Pioneer Accelerated Mortgage examines the marketing challenges that arise due to the unique characteristics of mortgage application processing. Process flow data and mortgage processing statistics are provided to the reader. Readers can also use primary market research information, in the form of summary survey data, to formulate adjustments for the company's marketing program.

It is important to point out that the cases presented in this book have been developed for pedagogical purposes only. As such, they are not intended to represent either good or poor management practice. The identities of the individuals and organizations named in these cases and associated figures, tables and locations have been altered for privacy and confidentiality purposes. The cases should be examined with the support of trained instructors who are familiar with the application of the key concepts covered. Readers are further encouraged to consult formal textbooks on marketing financial services to gain the background knowledge needed to address the questions posed in these cases.

SACRAMENTO FINANCIAL GROUP

It was 7am on a cool January morning and Janet Moss was already in the office hard at work, starting what she anticipated to be a long and difficult day. Moss was the product manager for commercial insurance products for Sacramento Financial Group (SFG). She was preparing material for a meeting with SFG's president, Stacey Anderson, to discuss expansion of SFG's operations into the consumer markets. Moss' pitch was going to be for a new product she was envisioning and had conveniently named HIT (Home Insurance for Tanks). Having worked at SFG for nearly 2 years and hoping for a promotion, Moss' presentation could have great impact on SFG's future, as well as her own career prospects.

SFG is a specialized financial services firm, focusing on commercial insurance and credit products. Located in Sacramento, CA, the company has a presence across the country and is a well-recognized name in the markets it serves. For example, SFG provides short-term loans to industrial companies, insures their equipment and product inventory, and provides motor vehicle insurance coverage for their vehicle fleets. In the conversations that morning, Moss said: *"Stacey Anderson has been putting a great deal of pressure on the entire company to find ways to grow, but I especially find my own team under a lot of pressure"*. She then continued: *"I am seeing a good level of growth in our tank removal financing for commercial and industrial accounts, which is great, but growth is also there in the tank leakage insurance protection products we sell to these customers. They are scared as hell when it comes to the financial burden of oil tank leakage, and this has been a big growth opportunity for us, and we've capitalized on it well"*. Moss then points to the stack of papers on her assistant's desk related to tank leakage insurance sales; she said she came in early this morning just so that she can process some of the mounting paperwork and also to begin to produce an executive presentation for Anderson on how to grow her group's business.

"While we are doing well selling tank leakage insurance to commercial accounts, I think there is a much greater untapped opportunity out there for us in consumer markets … you know your average homeowner who should be just as concerned about oil tank leakage from their home heating system. What we are seeing in the commercial markets is just the tip of the iceberg, and the iceberg is the private home market". Just a few weeks ago, Anderson had presented Moss and her team with a challenge to spend $50,000 to grow their business in an innovative way. Moss interpreted this move as Anderson's personal challenge to Moss, to see if Moss was worthy of a promotion within the company or at least some form of raise. Having graduated from a top business school in New York City only 18 months earlier, Moss felt that the presentation scheduled for the next day was not just a business discussion but also a personal test. *"No pressure"*, said Moss, while cracking into anxious laughter.

THE HISTORY AND CULTURE OF SACRAMENTO FINANCIAL GROUP

Sacramento Financial Group (SFG) was a large regional provider of financial solutions to commercial enterprises. It came to life in 1943 when two brothers, Sam and David Anderson, envisioned the creation of a specialized financial services firm to serve California's municipal governments' financing and insurance needs. At that time, when many banks and insurers shied away from California's municipalities due to their financial problems, SFG was one of the very few who helped specific local governments with their critical financial needs. SFG helped finance and insure the growth of many municipalities, and its unique ability to work with local governments, contractors and regulators enabled it to gradually grow its business to other states.   Having effectively served municipal government accounts, SFG began to serve commercial accounts, such as private manufacturers and distributors, in the 1960s.

Since its creation by the Anderson brothers, SFG has remained a family-owned entity.   Anderson family members hold most of the top management positions, including Stacey Anderson who is the youngest daughter of the late David Anderson.   Stacey Anderson's direct reports, Deborah Anderson and Michael Anderson, are her own children.   Michael Anderson, Moss's direct manager, is a 24 year old graduate from a local community college who had accumulated two years of sales experience in the cable industry before joining SFG six months earlier as the Vice President in charge of the insurance division.   Since the company is so family-focused, moving to the top was considered by many employees at SFG to be a family privilege, and the promotion of non-family members was only possible for unusually skilled and dedicated individuals.

Unlike its early days when municipal governments were its primary market, SFG's typical clients today are manufacturers, distributors and retailers nationwide.   The company has a total of 32,714 clients in all states (with the exception of Hawaii and Alaska, where it did not have any operations or clients due to regulatory constrains).   In the prior year, SFG was recognized as the 7th largest national financier in markets for manufacturing asset financing and the 11th largest insurer of manufacturing facilities nationwide.   SFG's organizational structure encompasses two major divisions: finance and insurance (organizational chart below).   Each division has multiple product managers who oversee a specific product family.   The Finance division provides credit solutions to commercial entities to help them finance the acquisition of assets such as machinery, motor vehicles, transportation equipment and office furniture.

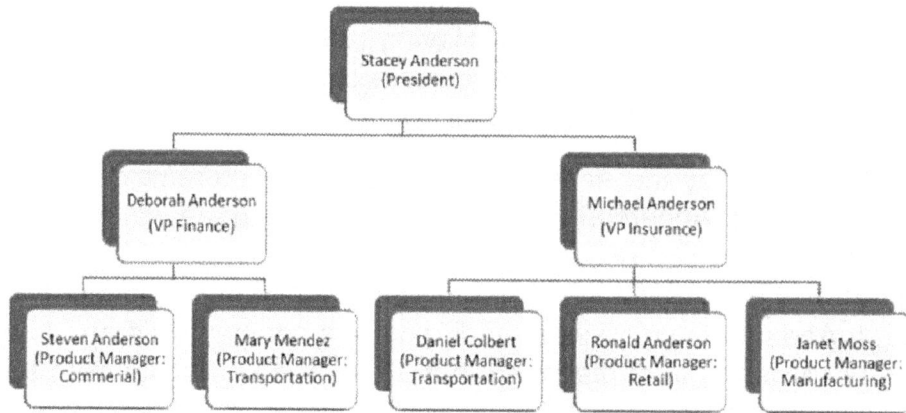

The Insurance division, on the other hand, focuses exclusively on insurance products for retailers, transportation companies and manufacturers. Moss was a product manager in the insurance division in charge of marketing insurance products catered to the needs of the manufacturing sector. Two other product managers in the insurance division dealt with insurance for transportation/distribution companies and for the retail sector. The insurance division covers several categories, but the most prominent are real estate insurance, insurance for equipment, auto insurance, liability insurance, and oil tank leakage insurance. The table below shows the distribution of some of the premium revenues sourced from different account types in the insurance division.

Insurance Business Line	Total Premiums Collected the Previous Year	Average Annual Growth in Premium Revenues Over the Last 5 Years
Real estate	$39,090,139	-0.2%
Equipment	$43,190,942	14.8%
Automobiles/vehicles	$10,390,091	1.37%
Liability	$909,830	-9.1%
Oil tank leakage	$1,628,839	18.7%

THE RISKS OF IN-GROUND OIL LEAKAGE

Crude oil and its byproducts, as well as other natural forms of oil, have been used as an energy source for thousands of years. The earliest uses of oil as an energy source date back to nearly 3000 BC and the invention of oil lamps during the Bronze Age for the production of light. Oil extracted from the fat content of hunted animals would be stored and then used in oil lamps and candles. Human use of oil as a source of energy had a major forward leap with the discovery of crude oil. While extraction of crude oil from the earth dates back to approximately 300 AD in China, large-scale extraction of crude oil only began in the late 1800s in Scotland, and quickly expanded worldwide. Since then, crude oil and its byproducts have made an abundant supply of energy available to mankind.

Extracted crude oil is processed in refineries to produce various petroleum products. These include gasoline, kerosene, aviation fuel, diesel fuel, propane and heating oil. Other byproducts of the refining process include lubricants, paraffin wax, tar and sulfur. These byproducts have many applications that are essential to the needs of industry and society. One of these – heating oil – has been the primary source of energy for residential and commercial heating applications in the United States for decades. The typical oil heating system requires a storage tank for the heating oil. This is because unlike natural gas and water, for which pipeline distribution systems exist within and between cities, no such pipelines can be safely set up for heating oil. As a result, each oil-powered heating system – whether commercial or residential – needs to have its own storage tank to store the amount of heating oil required to supply its boilers and burners.

The tanks that store heating oil can be placed over the ground (for example, next to a building) or underground (for example, underneath the soil in the yard in front of a building). Most buildings that use oil heating and were built prior to the mid-1970s have underground tanks. Underground tanks were first considered to be safe and sound by regulators. However, as tanks age and rust, and as the ground moisture surrounding the tanks affects their structural integrity, some can release oil into the ground. It is estimated that nearly 10% of underground tanks are at risk of leaking oil into the surrounding soil. Oil leakage not only translates into loss of oil reserves from the system but, more importantly, is extremely damaging to the environment. One way to know if a risk of release exists is to inject high-pressure air into the tank utilizing special equipment and examine if the tank is able to hold the pressure. If the tank is not able to hold the pre-specified internal pressure that is applied to it, its structural integrity may be compromised and it is at risk of releasing oil into the ground. Unfortunately, in most cases owners do not regularly conduct pressure tests and the tanks can suddenly release large amounts of oil into the ground without warning.

Federal, state and local laws impose significant penalties for property owners whose heating oil tanks leak. The property owner may also face law suits from private entities. This is because the release of heating oil into the earth contaminates surrounding water tables on a large scale and very quickly. The groundwater in surrounding areas may become unusable and the leakage can also create secondary threats to the environment, involving wildlife, rivers, streams and lakes. It is estimated that a one gallon release of heating oil into the earth can affect as much as one million gallons of ground water. Needless to say, over-ground tanks (those that are not placed in the earth) have a considerably lower risk of such issues, since the moisture from the earth and seismic forces that can compromise its structural integrity would not be present.

Due to the extreme risk presented by faulty in-ground oil tanks, any time there is an oil release, the remaining oil in the tank needs to be extracted, following which the tank is removed from the earth. Then, typically, a massive amount of soil (often in the orders of cubic tons) surrounding the tank needs to be removed. This process could translate to large financial outlays, ranging from $20,000 to hundreds of thousands of dollars. It is estimated that of the nearly 130 million homes and 6 million commercial building in the United States, about 10,000 in-ground oil releases occur each year.

WHAT IS "HIT"?

Similar to other forms of insurance such as auto and home insurance, the operator of an oil heating system with an in-ground oil tank can purchase oil tank leakage insurance protection from participating insurance companies. In the event of an oil leak, the insurer would cover some or all of the costs of the removal of the tank and the cleanup of the oil spill. Depending on the purchased insurance policy, limits to the coverage and terms of the insurance contract may apply.   For example, there are deductibles (typically $5,000), meaning that the first $5000 of costs would have to be paid by the policyholder. There are also caps, meaning that there is a maximum as to how much the insurance company would pay out in claims. The table below shows the typical premiums associated with a typical (500 gallon) tank for some of the companies that Moss considered as active competitors in the consumer residential markets.

	Monthly Premium	Policy details
Insurer A	$99	Deductible: $5,000 Maximum coverage: $50,000 Cost of new over-ground tank covered: No
Insurer B	$169	Deductible: $1,000 Maximum coverage: $150,000 Cost of new over-ground tank covered: Yes
Insurer C	$95	Deductible: $5,000 Maximum coverage: $20,000 Cost of new over-ground tank covered: No
Insurer D	$29	Deductible: $10,000 Maximum coverage: $20,000 Cost of new over-ground tank covered: No
Insurer E	$79	Deductible: $5,000 Maximum coverage: $50,000 Cost of new over-ground tank covered: No

Note: company names anonymized to protect their identities. Figures above are for 500 gallon tank.

Home Insurance for Tanks (HIT) was envisioned by Moss as a product aimed at homeowners across the country who have oil heating systems with in-ground oil tanks. Research estimated that nationally 27 million homes fall into this category and approximately 81% do not have tank leakage insurance protection. Moss believed this to be an untapped and sizable market, in which SFG could become a major player. In Moss' view, HIT should only focus on providing protection for in-ground oil tanks that are 500 gallons or smaller, which her assistant expected to constitute 66% of the 27 million homes with in-ground oil tanks. Moss believed the sub-500 gallon market is a safe zone for SFG to operate since larger tanks present greater financial risks for SFG in terms of potential cleanup costs if client claims are filed.

What Moss considered to be a unique selling proposition for HIT was what only one other competitor (Insurer B) provided – the additional coverage to provide a replacement over-ground tank once the in-ground tank has been removed. Moss noted that because of this unique feature, Insurer B not only has a strong market presence (she approximated 39% market share nationally), but also has been able to charge the highest premiums among all competitors in the market. The tank replacement component of HIT would pay for the installation of a new over-ground tank, in addition to the costs of removal of the old tank and the cleanup costs. Moss believed this to be the competitive advantage of SFG, as only one of the other competitors offered it. Moss believed that given the underlying risk of tank failures and the remediation costs for a typical tank failure, on average each HIT policy would cost SFG $288 per year to underwrite.

HIT'S FINANCIALS

For SFG's commercial accounts previously, established relationships had helped the company build new business. For example, a manufacturer that insured its production equipment with SFG may choose to insure its trucks as well. SFG also used a range of advertising options. In its early days print ads in business magazines, trade publications and newspapers were the primary means of advertising. In recent years it has had website banner ads on construction websites, postings on websites focusing on the manufacturing and transportation sectors, and social media campaigns that characterized SFG's communications efforts.

Since SFG had no prior experience with consumer markets, Moss had purchased a market research report, produced by a specialized consulting firm which profiled the tank insurance purchase decision process of homeowners. The study, which engaged a national sample of over 184 homeowners, profiled the decision making stages that homeowners go through when purchasing tank insurance policies. The research report estimated that 85% of homeowners do not even know such a risk exists. The research suggested that direct email and social media are the best approaches to make homeowners aware of the risk and to promote a specific insurance policy. It was estimated that of every 1,000 emails sent out to a target list of homeowners (costing approximately $2,500), 18 homeowners would be attracted so as to pay the attention to the message, and of those, 2 would eventually take steps to protect themselves through the purchase of a tank leakage insurance policy from the sender of the email. Another marketing approach used in the past by SFG was the use of full-page print ads in consumer publications. Though costs varied significantly from one publication to another, the typical ad would cost SFG about $20,000 and reach nearly 60,000 readers, resulting in about 35 leads of which 3 new customers would sign up. Moss had also considered hiring door-to-door sales people on a part-time basis. She estimated that a part-time employee, working for a 6 month time period would cost SFG about $40,000 (both salary and commissions) and would be able to present a sales pitch to approximately 600 homeowners in the given time period with a sign-up success rate of about 2%. The research also suggested that once a homeowner signs up for tank leakage protection, they will most likely keep the policy until they eventually sell the house, which the research firm estimated to be 12 years.

But "HIT is a different animal," Moss said. This is because HIT was an offering in the consumer (residential home market) in which SFG had never been involved. Also, Moss was concerned about the issue of consumer education: "Many homeowners do not even know that their underground oil tanks can leak, let alone know that they can buy HIT to protect themselves … it can be an uphill battle". She estimated that she would need to set up a special webpage and have special promotional material to educate prospective customers, and that this would cost her an additional $10,000 upfront. While she was very excited about the potential that HIT could bring to SFG, she believed the marketing effort required would be large, since much of the spending would have to focus on educating potential HIT customers on the underlying risks of in-ground tank failures. "They are sitting on a time bomb and they don't even know it", she said, and then continued: "I hope I am not sitting on a time bomb myself when it comes to the presentation to Stacey Anderson tomorrow! … I really need to think this through."

CASE QUESTION

What do you think Moss should recommend to Anderson in terms of how the $50,000 budget should be spent?

KR-20

"I have a great product but cannot seem to sell it!" protested Randy Griffin, the marketing manager for KR-20 at Kevin & Rogers (K&R). Griffin, who has been working his way up the corporate ladder at K&R, found this to be one of his more perplexing experiences in the nearly six years he has been with the firm. KR-20 is a credit checking service offered by K&R to loan officers at retail banks across the country. "Despite being attractively priced, no one wants it!" Griffin said. Having recently been put in charge of managing the marketing operations for KR-20, the poor market response was especially frustrating to Griffin, even more so because this was a product the top management considered both innovative and competitive. Yet the sales figures seemed to not match the excitement and expectations of top management, Griffin and outside observers.

PROCESSING OF PERSONAL LOAN APPLICATIONS

KR-20 was a service uniquely focusing on the needs of bank loan officers who regularly evaluate personal loan applications. Personal loans can, for example, be secured to purchase a car, remedy short-term cash flow issues or gain access to funds to satisfy household and family financial needs. To qualify for a personal loan, loan applicants need to provide bank loan officers with a series of personal and background information, such as their social security number, income information, credit history and employment status. These items are used by the loan officer to conduct the necessary background checks in order to determine if the applicant qualifies for a personal loan.

The loan application background checks assess the prospective borrower's financial standing, credit risk and creditworthiness. This process relies on two general sets of measures. The first set of measures are relatively easy to access, as they rely on the applicant's past credit history (typically available through one of the three major credit bureaus in the US) and assessment of personal wealth information (typically reflected in bank statements and investment holding reports submitted by the loan applicant). The second set of measures are more detailed and often require considerable footwork by the loan officer and bank staff. These include verification of current and past employment (which often requires contacting current and former employers) and criminal background checks (which require access to law enforcement databases). In addition, loan officers may conduct further background checks to examine the applicant's past business history and any public records which may assist in evaluating the creditworthiness of the applicant.

The workload associated with conducting background checks has grown over the years, making it a challenge for most loan officers to find the time and resources needed to properly vet the applications being received. This challenge is partially a result of the growing number of data sources that need to be consulted when assessing and verifying loan application information. Furthermore, the downsizing of bank operations in many retail banks in the United States has reduced the available staff to process loan applications carefully. Nevertheless, careless processing of loan applications can cause significant financial losses to banks, as loans may be issued to high-risk borrowers. At the same time, the increased processing time needed to carefully process application information could result in the loss of business, as prospective borrowers may seek to obtain loans from banks with speedier processing procedures.

Accurate and timely processing of personal loan applications are therefore critical to successful lending practices for all retail banks. Most of the large banks in the United States, such as those with national or regional presence, have centralized the processing of personal loans. Centralization is achieved by having a dedicated team of specialists, often working in the head office of the bank, processing the many applications received from the various bank branches. Loan officers would forward the loan application and associated documentation to the central office and request a full evaluation of the application.

The process was considerably less organized and highly decentralized for smaller local and community banks. Griffin estimated that there are nearly 5,000 such banks across the country, each with an average of 15 branches. According to him, these banks typically do not have the resources to centralize application processing operations and as a result, loan officers have to take on the task of conducting the necessary background checks themselves. The average time taken to process loan application information is about 5 hours per loan application for the typical loan officer, at an hourly pay rate of about $45. Griffin believed that on average each bank branch receives about 320 personal loan applications a year. Given the large number of applications, growing demands on loan officers' time and the reduced availability of staff in many local and community banks, outsourcing parts or all of the loan application process has become an attractive option.

KEVIN & ROGERS

KR-20 is one of many products and services that Kevin & Rogers (K&R) offered. K&R's primary business is account transfer processing for credit card companies. When credit card companies transfer their accountholders to another institution (often to a competing company in the form of bulk sale of credit card accounts), highly specialized administrative and information technology procedures are needed. K&R has several decades of experience, credibility and recognition in this line of work, which now accounts for nearly 70% of the company's revenues. K&R also provides consulting services for retail banks that are re-organizing or are in need of specialized legal advice on regulatory compliance matters. In recent years K&R entered the business of advising banks on credit background checks– a business opportunity that arose through K&R's consulting work with several community banks in the Midwest. This opportunity eventually transformed into a standardized and formalized service, which the company's co-CEO named "KR-20," as the product launch decision was made on his daughter's 20th birthday.

Shortly thereafter, Kevin & Rogers acquired a small Colorado based IT firm specializing in algorithmic processing of social media and financial datasets, making KR-20 a commercially viable and competitive offering. Access to these algorithms made it possible for Kevin & Rogers to gain an edge over competitors by being able to more methodically and efficiently process loan application information. Despite the competitive advantages gained from this acquisition, Kevin & Rogers continues to struggle with name recognition in the loan application processing business, as it is better known for the other services it offers in the financial services sector.

THE KR-20 OFFERING

Kevin & Rogers is one of only four national providers of personal loan application processing services. The company's KR-20 product competes with similar services offered by three established competitors in the business – all of whom have decades more experience in this marketplace. All these companies provide loan officers the ability to delegate the full task of conducting the background checks and providing preliminary assessment of the loan application, for a fee. The exhibit below shows the market share of the four products in this marketplace.

Kredit Chex	38%
Good2Lend	35%
FreezFacts	24%
KR-20	3%

Like the competing products, KR-20 is a service that provides loan officers with the applicant's credit history, wealth information, employment profile and criminal background checks. In addition to these standard measures, however, Kevin & Rogers' acquisition of the Colorado-based IT firm provided it with the ability to provide loan officers with additional layers of information that could assist them in their loan issuance decisions. These included KR-20's use of a patented computer algorithm that examines the application and identifies high-risk applicants. In addition, KR-20 uses a specialized web-crawling software that scans social media and general internet sites to measure the public profile of the loan applicant. This measure helps associate each loan applicant with pre-existing categories of borrowers, which can inform loan officers of the projected credit risk profile of the applicant.

Furthermore, in order to expedite and economize the employment history verification process, Kevin & Rogers has partnered with an overseas firm who can conduct the necessary verification tasks at a fraction of the cost of US-based alternatives. As a result, the overall cost to Kevin & Rogers for processing a typical loan application was approximately $18. A recent study conducted by an independent research firm indicated that KR-20 was 28% more accurate than the industry average in identifying high-risk loan applicants. The same study also revealed that KR-20 reports are generated with an average of 18 hours of loan officer requests, compared to the industry average of 31 hours.

The pricing of KR-20 depends on the bank branch's level of use of the service, as shown in the table below. Each bank branch would be billed directly based on the number of loan requests they expect to make every year, and the billing adjustment for the actual number of loan applications processed each year would be done at the end of the year. The pricing structure for the competing products was less flexible and did not vary as a function of the number of loan applications processed.

Number of Loan Applications Per Year	KR-20 Price (per application)
1-50	$49
51-99	$39
100 or more	$29

Kredit Chex which offered similar services (but lacked the social media web crawling feature of KR-20) was priced at $85 per application and had a guaranteed 4-day turnaround. Good2Lend was priced at $45 per application but offered no job verification or web-crawling features to loan officers. It did not provide any guaranteed turnaround time period. FeezFacts did not offer a package but offered each individual component that a loan officer may wish to obtain to form his/her own assessment: $25 for credit background check and $35 for a criminal background check. The loan officer using FeezFacts would then have to conduct his/her own employment verification and carry out a web search to assess the loan applicant's online profile in social media and other websites (this would typically take a loan officer or bank staff about 2 hours).

ISSUES INHIBITING KR-20'S GROWTH

Griffin's frustration was evident in his words, cited earlier. Believing KR-20 to be a good product, he was baffled by its small footprint in the marketplace. He was also frustrated by the lack of understanding and sympathy from the top management at K&R in appreciating the complexity of the loan application processing marketplace. One of the areas of concern for Griffin was the choice of the product name: KR-20. To him, KR-20 did not seem to communicate its purpose well and sounded more like the name of a chemical agent used in manufacturing or industrial applications. He pointed out that competitors use brand names (rather than numeric designations), which may appeal more to loan officers. He was also frustrated that top management did not support KR-20 by allocating sufficient promotional funds. For the most part, the product was cross-sold to the Chief Marketing Officers of banks with which K&R had business relations. At the beginning of the previous year, Griffin oversaw the launch of an advertising campaign costing $27,500. This campaign secured a Gross Rating Point of 35,000 units and reached nearly 21,000 loan officers nationwide. By the end of the year, Griffin estimated that of all the loan officers reached through this campaign, approximately 150 had commenced using KR-20 consistently and continuously for all their loan applications.

Another issue of concern was the pricing of KR-20. It was unclear to him what an optimal price for KR-20 should be, and whether the price should be lowered or increased, and if so by how much. This, combined with the confusing name, made the task of communicating the service to loan officers challenging.   He also believed loan officers typically do not embrace change, and if they are already using the products of one of the three competitors, it would take a great deal of convincing before they would give KR-20 a shot. Griffin's concerns were further complicated by the fact that Kevin & Rogers was not a known name to many loan officers around the country. Regulatory concerns were also at play in the coming year or two. Specifically, the top two competitors were considering merging their loan application processing subsidiaries. The potential merger was being examined very carefully by the federal government for its possible anti-trust implications. Such a merger would clearly change the competitive landscape and the success prospects for KR-20.

CASE QUESTIONS

1. Compute the expected Herfindhal Index for this market, if the merger described in this case takes place, and explain what this index implies in terms of the state of the competition.
2. What is your assessment of the ad campaign described in this case?
3. What are your recommendations to Griffin regarding the potential renaming of KR-20?
4. What would you consider to be the optimal price for KR-20?
5. Which existing federal regulations may prevent the merger of the two competitors discussed in the case?

FARMERS BANK OF VIRGINIA

COMPANY BACKGROUND

At a regularly scheduled Friday meeting of the top executives of Farmers Bank of Virginia (FBV) in Richmond, VA, an atmosphere of confusion and frustration permeated the room. The board meeting, which was scheduled for two hours, had gone over time and was well into its fourth hour of heated deliberations. At stake was the future identity of a bank that for decades had been a trusted name among all the Virginian communities it served. Farmers Bank of Virginia was established in 1924 by George Capaccio. Capaccio, an Italian immigrant that had volunteered to serve with the American forces in World War I, was a strong believer in traditional values and the importance of keeping a strong foundation in every element of his life, including the many successful businesses he helped launch and manage. For example, in the 1920s, many competing banks participated in both commercial and investment banking activities. Capaccio, however, believed that the deposits made by his customers were not to be played with in the high-stakes game of investment banking. He therefore persuaded the bank's board of directors to steer most of the bank's assets away from investment banking and to engage only in investments that were deemed safe. "We should treat customer deposits with the respect we'd give our own families' life savings, and make sure we do one thing and do it damn well," he mentioned at the 1927 annual meeting with the bank's employees.

As a result of Capaccio's traditional approach, FBV was considered one of the strongest and most stable community banks in the east coast, especially during the late 1920s and early 1930s when many competing banks began to fold. The bank's customers always appreciate the stability and discipline that Capaccio brought to the bank, and many of them stayed with the bank throughout their entire lives. Most of their children and future generations also became loyal bank customers, creating an image of tradition and strength for FBV. The bank eventually grew from a single branch in Richmond to 32 branches throughout various locations in Virginia. FBV was praised by many for providing the best personalized service in the retail banking business. Small-town values and the personal touch were key driving forces in the marketing efforts of the bank, and the bank prided itself on the relationships with its customers that developed over the years. The bank employed nearly 500 people. Approximately 124,000 FBV customers primarily used it for checking and savings purposes, and the bank was largely viewed by the communities it served as a safe place to deposit funds.

EMERGING TRENDS

Despite the strong traditions and loyal customers that had characterized FBV's experience over the years, change was occurring everywhere. Due to deregulation and mergers, the emerging picture for all banks in the US, and especially for small community banks such as FBV, was one of intense competition and limited innovation and creativity. Anne Bagozzi, the Vice President of Marketing, had been assigned by the board of directors to identify the bank's overall marketing strategy for the next several years. Bagozzi, who was the granddaughter of Capaccio, felt a strong sense of responsibility to make sure that Capaccio's principles would be a core part of the bank's future strategy. As an ex-medic who had served in Vietnam, she knew the demands of a quickly changing environment and the need for rapid response. Yet her three decades of service with the bank had typically been far from the experiences of the battlefields of Vietnam, and she questioned at times the bank's ability to mobilize in new and untested territories.

To reinvent itself, the bank had taken on some new directions in recent years. A new ad campaign was designed to communicate the core values of the company and its long history and tradition of customer care. Slogans such as "The bank you can trust ..." and "Old time values ..." were featured in both print and broadcast ads. In the last two years alone, FBV had spent nearly a half million dollars on these ads. They also hired an outside consulting firm to develop the specs for moving the bank into the mobile banking platform. Although FBV's online banking features were fully functional, its mobile banking services were not yet operational. FBV also expanded its automated teller machine (ATM) network by providing additional ATM devices in its 32 bank branches. It was mandated by the top management that all bank branches have at least two operational ATM devices. Fifteen (15) of these branches also had an additional drive-through ATM for use by motorists.

Reflecting on the bank's current situation, Bagozzi noted, "Even credit card companies and insurance agents are fighting for our business ... it's ridiculous who we have to deal with ... the next thing you know, we'll have to compete with the local convenience store." In addition to the new competitors springing up, an additional concern of Bagozzi was the changing picture of the typical customer:

"Up until about a decade ago, we had a very good feel for who we were serving. Most of our customers had their parents and grandparents banking with us as well. Back then, when we conducted a series of focus groups, we had found that some of our older customers even remembered their grandparents talking about what my grandfather had done to ensure the safety and security of their life savings. The strength of the bank and its

traditions were with us, decades after the fact. But today, I'm not sure who the customers are. The older customers are getting older and doing less of the types of transactions we'd like them to do. Many have retired and even moved down south, and we now have a new breed of customers, younger and affluent, but different from those we served less than a decade ago."

	Census 10 Years Ago	Current Census Data
Average household income (in current dollars)	$58,820	$71,259
Average age	36.5	34.7
Percent of population over the age of 65	35%	31%
Percent of population with college degrees	19%	27%

To better understand the trends, Bagozzi referred to demographic data and how the population had changed based on census information within a 3-mile radius of the bank's 32 branch locations (exhibit above). This form of analysis would provide a general feel for the way in which the population base in the surrounding areas of the branches had evolved.

Bagozzi conceded that FBV's understanding of who the customers are and what they want is somewhat limited. *"It's fuzzy science right now, and I hope we can quickly get a feel for where we should be going ... we don't know who they are and what they want now, let alone five years from now,"* she said. The board of directors gave her a mandate to develop a 5-year strategy for the bank and to do so before the end of the year – a tough task, even for a former war-time medic.

A few months earlier Bagozzi had hired Jill Banner as her assistant in charge of strategic marketing. Banner, 29, had worked for five years as a marketing manager for an upstart online broker in Washington, D.C. Banner then completed her MBA with a concentration in marketing and joined FBV shortly after graduation. As one of six people reporting directly to Bagozzi, Banner would be responsible for all elements of market research, business planning, and overall administration needed to design and implement the new face of the bank.

Having been on the job for less than a month, Banner had commented in a weekly meeting with Bagozzi that the general image of the bank needed to be shifted:

> *"I know the bank has its traditions and values, but the general direction of the bank is simply not appealing to me and people in my age bracket. I mean even the name of the bank with "farmers" being part of it. When was the last time you saw a farmer walking in Richmond, or see one go into one of our branches?"*

In fact, Banner believed that, not only did the bank have to change its products and services, but that it should also change its name and do a complete rebuilding of its image. She wanted to build a new bank from the ground up. Bagozzi, despite her enthusiasm over hiring a young energetic executive, was uncomfortable about the drastic changes she proposed. Bagozzi's gut feeling was that the bank should capitalize on the segment of its customers that was affluent, move up-market, and engage in higher margin activities such as investment services and financial advising. She was reluctant to move the bank away from its traditional strengths and to abandon her grandfather's principle, which for decades had guided the bank through rough waters. She therefore asked Banner to arrange a series of market research studies to help both of them better understand their customers and to use this information in order to strategize their next steps.

SECONDARY MARKET RESEARCH

Banner's first step was to conduct a thorough examination of secondary data sources. She also consulted various national organizations and regulatory bodies who normally collect useful data and monitor bank activities, such as the Federal Deposit Insurance Corporation (FDIC) and the Federal Reserve. Many of the points that Bagozzi had mentioned to her turned out to be true. For example, Banner found that a decade earlier, 18 banks competed with FBV in its top three markets. The number had since dropped to 7 due to the consolidations and mergers that had been commonplace among banks in Virginia, especially in the previous three years. She also found that five of these seven banks offered free checking accounts to new customers, while FBV still offered a series of fee-based checking account choices. Banner's study of the bank's own records also showed some disturbing trends that she found surprising, especially since no one, not even Bagozzi, had been aware of them. For example, the number of customers that the bank served had consistently dropped in the past 5 years, but a notable decline was evident in the very last year − a drop of approximately 9% in its customer base. More importantly, this trend did not seem to be true of FBV's leading competitors.

While this decline was probably not sufficiently large to sound any major alarms, it was unclear why such a dramatic drop had occurred. Banner had also noted that, out of the seven competing banks, six provided mobile banking and, out of these six, only one charged additional fees for this service.

Banner also sent out several mystery shoppers to understand the flavor of the competing banks' offerings. The mystery shoppers were mostly her college friends who were doing this work for her as a favor. They spent considerable time going to branches of each of the seven competing banks. In their observations, they noted that most of the competing branches offered customer service that was much less personalized and less accessible than what FBV offered. Long teller lines and relatively cold teller interactions were typical of these banks, and the prices charged for relatively standard services were somewhat confusing. In fact, when looking at the prices for the competing banks' services, it seemed that, while checking services were offered for free, some of the banks might charge special fees for visiting a bank teller or calling the bank's customer service phone lines. This was true of three of the seven banks. They did, however, notice that these competing banks offered a much wider array of financial services to their customers. For example, almost all offered some form of insurance product and prominently featured them in brochures available at the branches. Two of these banks had also set up investment service offices at their branch locations.

PRIMARY MARKET RESEARCH

Unconvinced that the available research would provide the full scope of information needed to make the necessary strategic decisions, Bagozzi and Banner contacted Financial Research Associated Solutions (FRAS), a market research company specialized in financial services marketing, to conduct two waves of primary research studies. The first wave consisted of eight focus groups with both customers and non-customers of the bank. The focus groups were designed by FRAS to better understand how people perceived the bank and what customer needs were not currently being met by FBV. The second wave of research by FRAS used consumer surveys conducted at several shopping malls in the vicinity of several FBV branch locations. The surveys were intended to help test and quantify some of the observations made through the focus groups.

FOCUS GROUP FINDINGS

A total of eight focus groups were conducted in a two-month time period. The focus groups were held in two central locations where FRAS operated specialized focus group facilities. Half of the focus groups were existing FBV customers and the other half were non-customers. The focus group sessions were further split by age. Half of the focus groups were conducted with individuals below the age of 45 and the other half were conducted with individuals 45 and older. As a result, a total of four categories of focus group sessions were carried out, with each category consisting of two focus group sessions.

	Below the age of 45	45 years old and older
FBV Customers	Image of FBV: - Family oriented - Old - Slow Strength: - Name I can trust - Security - Orderly Weakness: - Technology - Slow service - Narrow range of products Additional Services Needed: - Insurance - Investment services - More flexible loan policy	Image of FBV: - Family oriented - Traditional - Trustworthy Strength: - Name I can trust - Orderly - Security Weakness: - Narrow range of products - Limited parking space - No weekend hours Additional Services Needed: - Investment services - Financial advice - Wider choice of home loans
Non-Customers	Image of FBV: - Old - Slow - Archaic Strength: - Traditional - Security - Name I can trust Weakness: - Lack of mobile banking - Technology - Need to use tellers Additional Services Needed: - Mobile banking - Insurance - Auto loans	Image of FBV: - Trustworthy - Family oriented - Old Strength: - Security - Name I can trust - Stable business Weakness: - Old systems - No weekend hours - Slow service Additional Services Needed: - Financial advice - Home mortgages - Investment services

The focus groups were moderated by a consumer research specialist at FRAS who had conducted qualitative research on bank marketing for over a decade. The moderator discussed several issues related to the customers' views of FBV, specifically related to the image of the bank, its perceived strengths and weaknesses, and new services which they thought might best meet their needs. These responses were then categorized and tabulated by the moderator and two assistant researchers at FRAS, and the most frequently mentioned responses are shown in the exhibit above.

CONSUMER SURVEYS

Following the focus group sessions, a series of surveys were administered in shopping malls at various locations nearby several key FBV branches. The company believed the shopping public in these locations would be representative of the customer profiles that each bank branch attempts to attract. The survey did not focus on FBV in particular but probed individual consumers' views of the kinds of services that they believed to be important in the operations of a bank branch. Importance ratings were obtained using a 1-to-5 scale, with 1 being "not important" and 5 being "very important."

A total of 368 surveys were administered during early November. The results were subsequently tabulated, analyzed using statistical software, and dissected into two groups of consumers, those below the age of 45, and those 45 and older. The exhibit below reports the results. The reported figures are top-box percentages, which reflect the percentage of respondents in each age category who believed the item to be "very important" by rating it a 5 on the 1-to-5 importance scale.

	Below the age of 45	45 years old and older
Weekend operations	35%	54%
Availability of mobile banking	67%	34%
Friendly teller service	43%	68%
Wide ATM network	71%	57%
Convenient branch locations	23%	63%
Availability of parking	37%	68%
Well-lit parking and branch location	32%	71%
Well-decorated branches	18%	21%
Knowledgeable staff	39%	57%
Availability of investment services	15%	71%
Availability of insurance products and services	57%	52%
Availability of mortgages	24%	53%
Free checking	79%	77%

THE DECISION

Bagozzi and Banner began preparing for their presentation of a 5-year strategic plan. Having spent nearly $170,000 on marketing research, the quality of their advice would not only be important to the future of their own professional status within the bank, but also to the long-term survival of FBV.

CASE QUESTIONS

1. What objectives do you think should be included in the 5-year strategic plan for FBV?

2. Provide a timeline of the activities needed to achieve the objectives you have identified.

ASSETSGUARD

It was a Friday evening in late December. At the headquarters of *InsuOn.com* in White Plains, New York, most of the company's 85 employees were getting ready for the Christmas season. Many had been spending part of their time shopping for gifts and organizing a big office Christmas party to be held later that night to celebrate the company's third Christmas. However, the spirit of Christmas had not yet found its way to the cubicle of Christopher Winer, the Executive Vice President of Marketing. Winer had the challenging task of making several key decisions over the weekend that could affect the entire future of InsuOn and all of its employees.

Winer's challenge was to decide how to strategically introduce an identity theft insurance policy called AssetsGuard. This was a considerable deviation from InsuOn's traditional insurance product lines, which primarily consisted of term life insurance and traveler's insurance policies. Nevertheless, the opportunity to move into what seemed to be a fast-growing market was difficult to ignore. Identity theft occurs when an individual obtains access to personal information such as a person's credit card number or social security number and uses this information to either obtain access to credit or to misidentify himself. Three forms of identity theft are known to occur frequently. The first is criminal identity theft, which occurs when a criminal that has been confronted by law enforcement does not provide them with his own real name, but proceeds to provide another individual's name. As a result, criminal records and arrest warrants would be issued to the name of the individual that was named, rather than the individual apprehended by law enforcement.

A somewhat similar form of identity theft is referred to as identity cloning; this involves the use of an individual's personal information by a criminal to establish for himself a completely new identity. This act involves the use of the individual's name and personal information to obtain a social security number, driver's license, or other critical documents that identify an individual in modern day society.

The third form of identity theft is referred to as financial identity theft (FIT). FIT involves the use of a victim's name or social security number by the criminal in order to obtain access to credit from a financial institution. For example, using this personal information, the criminal could apply for a credit card and use the card for personal purchases. The victim would be footed with the bill, unless an appeal was made to the credit card company. While most credit card companies have their own protection plans to cover potential losses due to FIT, the growing occurrence of FIT had begun to cause considerable alarm among consumers and regulators. Some estimated that every year, about 2.8% of the population in the United States would be affected by identity theft, and that the cost of reversing the damaging effects of FIT, in terms of legal fees, lost wages, and administrative expenses would typically range between $500 and $1,500 per case. AssetsGuard was InsuOn's response to the explosive growth in financial identity theft cases.

COMPANY BACKGROUND

InsuOn (short for Insurance Online) was founded in 1997 by Joseph Wilson. Wilson, who as a young adult never had the financial resources to attend college, joined a Fortune 500 information technology company after graduating from high school. He worked his way up from mailroom clerk to computer programmer. His technical skills and his outgoing personality eventually helped him move up the ranks; at the age of 28, he was one of the top 15 managers in the company. At around that time, Wilson decided to leave the corporate world. Capitalizing on the Internet boom, he set up his own company—InsuOn.com. InsuOn started off as a distributor of term-life insurance products to teachers, university professors, scientists, and educators in New York, New Jersey, and Connecticut. In the first year of its operations, the company sold nearly 12,000 policies, far exceeding even the most aggressive projections. Within four years, this figure had nearly tripled to 34,500 policyholders.

The fast growth of the company, which led to the issuance of an IPO (initial public offering), created an infusion of funds needed to support the company's growth. InsuOn quickly expanded to providing traveler's insurance, which was primarily sold online through travel agencies as well as directly to individual consumers. The company also expanded its Internet offering of term-life insurance beyond just teachers and educators, and it also expanded coverage to five additional states, mostly on the east coast.

Wilson's philosophy on running a successful business was largely based in his own personal values and life beliefs. He believed that, in many business transactions, the middleman does not add any value to the customer experience, but is primarily there to take away cash from both the seller and the buyer. He often cited examples such as GEICO, a direct marketer of property and casualty insurance that, by skipping the middleman, has been able to challenge the traditional models by which insurance companies had operated for decades; however, it also provides good service and attractive prices to its customers. According to Wilson, many insurance markets were becoming commoditized, and the true differences between the various brands were diluting. Automotive insurance, term life insurance, homeowners insurance, and travelers insurance were, in his opinion, the types of products that do not need personal selling and can be sold with little or no human interaction. "All you need is a good website and nice people on the customer service phone line," he once told Winer. Wilson was also a strong believer in breaking down barriers within his own organization. For example, he believed that top executives in the company should not be treated differently than other employees; they too should have cubicles, not their own offices, and park in the regular employee parking lot rather than in reserved spots. On the floor where InsuOn operated in White Plains, no one, including Wilson and Winer, had their own personal office. Wilson believed that, by following such an organizational model, one broke down the barriers that separate management from the rest of the company and created a much more communicative and efficient work environment.

ASSETSGUARD

While Wilson's philosophy of cost efficiencies was crucial to the company's early successes with term life and travelers insurance markets, the competitive nature of these markets had limited InsuOn's contribution margin to about 38%. Wilson was under considerable pressure from InsuOn investors and industry analysts to move the margins up, and the goal was to secure margins of 45% or higher for most of the company's new products. Wilson's new idea of providing identity theft insurance may have been just the solution for this goal. AssetsGuard was a unique form of protection against financial identity theft. While identity theft insurance was beginning to be offered by some of the major property and casualty insurance companies, public awareness of the availability of this service was altogether very limited. A survey conducted by a Washington–based lobbying group had shown that less than 30% of the population was even aware of the existence of identity theft insurance products. Moreover, Wilson noticed that competing identity theft insurance policies offered by the major insurance companies provided very specific levels of coverage. For example, for a premium of $14.99 a month, an individual could obtain coverage for up to $20,000. This would be the maximum amount for which the insurer would protect the policyholder. The policy would cover the costs of legal fees that attorneys might charge for reversing the effects of FIT on the policyholder's financial and credit records. It would also cover up to $2,500 (as part of the maximum $20,000 coverage) of lost wages in case the policyholder had to attend court hearings related to the FIT case. Insurance agents nationally provided similar policies with nearly identical coverage in the $12.99/month to $39.99/month range.

AssetsGuard was a considerably different type of FIT insurance. While the competing FIT insurance policies had specific amounts and conditions of coverage, Wilson believed that distressed consumers victimized by identity theft should not be bothered by policy limits, terms and conditions. He personally had designed the product to carry new, attractive features. For example, in case of identity theft, AssetsGuard would cover the policyholder for up to $40,000, which was a much higher coverage level than what the majority of competing policies offered. In addition, the entire face value of $40,000 would be available to the policyholder to retain the services of a pre-defined network of attorneys specialized in FIT with whom InsuOn had established relationships. As a result, the policyholder would neither have to pay an attorney out of pocket, nor subsequently have to file for, and await, claim payments. The availability of a specialized network of attorneys also helped ease possible policyholder anxieties. AssetsGuard also conducted monthly checks of policyholder credit reports to monitor potential cases of FIT and to alert the policyholder. This was a truly unique feature of the product that, in combination with the generous and well-organized structure of the policy, would relieve most concerns and anxieties an individual might have regarding financial identity theft.

Similar to InsuOn's other insurance products, AssetsGuard would be sold through the company's web site. Wilson also envisioned promoting the product to financial advisors, who would in turn recommend it to their clients. The expected launch date for AssetsGuard was March of the coming year, giving Winer less than 100 days to plan the launch and to set up the infrastructure and marketing programs needed to support it. Winer estimated that the incremental cost of expanding the web site and hiring additional staff to support AssetsGuard would be approximately $650,000 a year; an additional $400,000 a year would be needed for the first two years to fund related advertising campaigns. Having been in the business of selling insurance for nearly three decades and 12 years senior to Wilson, Winer was not fully convinced that Wilson's idea would be well received by the market.

CONSUMER RESEARCH

Only 6 weeks ago, in early November, Winer had attended three focus groups on AssetsGuard commissioned by the company. The focus groups, held in Boston, were attended by panels of consumers. The attendees were heads of households with annual household incomes in the $100,000-$249,999 range who owned their residential property. Winer believed this to be a representative target group for those who might be interested in purchasing FIT insurance policies. The focus groups were moderated and conducted by a research company specializing in insurance marketing. The sessions were designed such that, at the beginning, participants were queried on their general knowledge of identity theft and companies they know that provide identity theft insurance or might provide it in the future. They were then given the description for AssetsGuard and asked for their opinions. Open-ended conversations then followed and, at the end, their recall of the AssetsGuard name, its policy description, and price expectations were measured using a short questionnaire. Each participant was paid $75 for attending.

The consumer research results revealed that most of the participants in all three focus group sessions were unaware that identity theft insurance policies even existed. Of the 27 individuals who participated in the focus group sessions, only five claimed to have known that such insurance policies exist. When asked which companies they believed would be good providers of such insurance policies, the most frequently mentioned companies were established insurers that had agent organizations and were active in both property and casualty and life insurance markets. The second most frequently mentioned group of companies were the major commercial banks. Finally, some participants believed that their mortgage companies might also be trustworthy providers of identity theft insurance. In the second phase of each focus group session, participants were engaged in open-ended conversations about the value they saw in the features of the AssetsGuard policy. These discussions revealed that the focus group participants found the benefits to be highly attractive and beneficial to their peace of mind. An unrelated task followed in order to distract the participants for approximately 10 minutes, following which recall measures and price estimates were obtained (this is common practice in consumer research to help measure consumer memory).

After the distraction task, participants were given a short questionnaire that asked them to recall the name of the insurance policy that had been presented to them earlier and to provide an estimate of the monthly premiums that they think would be reasonable. Of the 27 participants, only 14 could remember the exact name of AssetsGuard. Other names mentioned were "AssetCard", "FastGuard" and "LastGuard". As for the question on monthly premiums, the average for the 27 participants was $28.32, but the figure ranged from a low of $18 to a high of $48. Half of the participants did not see sufficient need for purchasing such an insurance policy. The questionnaire concluded with an open-ended question that asked the participants to point out any reservations they had about buying a policy such as AssetsGuard. The most frequently mentioned concern was the need to purchase identity theft insurance. The second most frequently mentioned concern was that the existing insurance policies that the person had, such as homeowners insurance, might already cover FIT. Finally, some participants were concerned with using the Internet to purchase identity theft insurance. This is especially a concern as a significant amount of identity theft takes place over the Internet. Many of these participants were also concerned about the process of the online sale of a policy such as AssetsGuard, which would involve no face-to-face contact, and questioned the trustworthiness of such a transaction.

Though the focus group results provided Winer with a first-hand feel for market response to the AssetGuard concept, he requested additional information from the research provider, such as the expected cost of various media he could use to advertise and promote AssetsGuard and the resulting conversion rate, which reflects the probability that a given consumer targeted with the ad would sign up for the policy. While the research provider was not able to provide exact estimates, general ball-park figures were provided (exhibit below). In addition, the research company conducted a survey of 60 competitors in various regions by profiling their prices for policies with coverage similar to AssetsGuard. Based on filings with state insurance commissioners and a statistical model, the research company produced a table of conversion rates, reflecting their estimates of the percentage of customers targeted with the insurance product at a given price who were likely to subscribe (exhibit below). In this exhibit, CPM reflects the cost of reaching out to a target audience of one thousand individuals, and conversion rate reflects the probability that an individual who has observed the ad will purchase the promoted product.

Target Audience	Medium	CPM	Conversion Rate
Non-customers	Direct mail	$25-$35	0.020%-0.050%
Non-customers	Radio advertising	$32-$47	0.050%-0.075%
Non-customers	Cable TV advertising	$68-$91	0.115%-0.145%
Existing customers	Direct mail	$25-$35	0.190%-0.350%
Existing customers	Telemarketing	$98-$125	2.25%-3.15%

In addition, the research company conducted a survey of 60 competitors in various regions by profiling their prices for policies with coverage similar to AssetsGuard. Based on filings with state insurance commissioners and a statistical model, the research company produced a table of conversion rates, reflecting their estimates of the percentage of customers targeted with the insurance product at a given price who were likely to subscribe (exhibit below). In this exhibit, the conversion rate reflects the probability estimates produced by the research company, that an individual who is presented with the insurance product at a given price and coverage level by the identified competitor will subscribe to it.

Competitor	Price	Coverage Level	Conversion Rate	Competitor	Price	Coverage Level	Conversion Rate	Competitor	Price	Coverage Level	Conversion Rate
1	$19.95	$5,000	1.8%	21	$19.95	$1,500	1.7%	41	$29.95	$750	0.2%
2	$14.95	$2,000	9.9%	22	$12.95	$2,500	6.9%	42	$29.95	$1,500	0.2%
3	$19.95	$1,500	1.7%	23	$10.95	$750	9.7%	43	$12.95	$5,000	7.2%
4	$29.95	$2,500	0.2%	24	$29.95	$2,500	0.2%	44	$12.95	$1,500	6.8%
5	$29.95	$1,500	0.2%	25	$9.95	$10,000	13.7%	45	$9.95	$1,500	11.8%
6	$10.95	$750	9.7%	26	$29.95	$2,500	0.2%	46	$9.95	$5,000	12.6%
7	$10.95	$5,000	9.5%	27	$41.95	$2,500	0.0%	47	$9.95	$2,500	12.0%
8	$10.95	$2,500	10.0%	28	$12.95	$2,500	6.9%	48	$29.95	$1,500	0.2%
9	$10.95	$1,500	9.8%	29	$10.95	$1,500	9.8%	49	$10.95	$2,500	10.0%
10	$54.95	$1,500	0.1%	30	$10.95	$1,500	9.8%	50	$12.95	$5,000	7.2%
11	$54.95	$2,000	0.2%	31	$19.95	$2,500	1.7%	51	$12.95	$2,500	6.9%
12	$12.95	$5,000	7.2%	32	$29.95	$2,500	0.2%	52	$19.95	$1,500	1.7%
13	$10.95	$2,500	10.0%	33	$19.95	$1,500	1.7%	53	$10.95	$10,000	9.5%
14	$29.95	$1,500	0.2%	34	$10.95	$5,000	9.1%	54	$41.95	$1,500	0.0%
15	$29.95	$2,500	0.2%	35	$9.95	$10,000	10.7%	55	$19.95	$750	1.7%
16	$41.95	$5,000	0.0%	36	$41.95	$3,000	0.1%	56	$29.95	$10,000	0.3%
17	$54.95	$750	0.1%	37	$29.95	$5,000	0.2%	57	$19.95	$750	1.7%
18	$10.95	$1,500	9.8%	38	$10.95	$1,500	9.8%	58	$10.95	$5,000	8.5%
19	$19.95	$1,500	1.7%	39	$9.95	$1,500	11.8%	59	$10.95	$1,500	9.8%
20	$54.95	$5,000	0.2%	40	$19.95	$2,500	1.7%	60	$13.95	$3,000	7.2%

WINER'S DECISION

Winer's time for deciding had arrived. He not only had to make a strategic decision on whether to launch AssetsGuard or not but also had to determine the details of the pricing and promotion plan. While Wilson questioned the product's potential, he also wondered about the brand name and its fit to what the product was truly intended to represent. His traditional training as an economist conflicted with the inspirations and pragmatic style of Wilson, who seemed keen on InsuOn's venture into this little known territory of the insurance world.

CASE QUESTION

Should AssetsGuard be launched?

LIBERTY ASSET FINANCING

In a confidential staff meeting, Donna Sanchez, the marketing manager for Liberty Asset Financing (LAF), expressed her many concerns about the future of the business and the potential downfalls that it would face if her staff did not actively innovate. She oversaw a payroll of nearly 80 employees, including administrative staff located in the LAF head office in Bethesda, Maryland and sales specialists located across the country. While business may have been too slow to even discuss growth, LAF's Board of Directors gave a mandate to all senior managers to focus on growth and to counter the downward market trends of the time by building long-term capabilities and establishing new footholds in markets where LAF operated.

Liberty Asset Financing was established to provide customized financial services to small and medium sized industrial companies as well as to distributors who carry their products. For example, when a furniture manufacturer would sell a large volume of products to a retailer or distributor, LAF would take on the task of providing credit for the transaction and financing the sale. This not only helped the manufacturer to focus on its core strength – manufacturing – but it also brought large volumes of financing business for LAF. The close relationship between manufacturers, distributors and LAF enabled it to generate large profit streams during good economic times. In the past three years, however, LAF's volume of business had dropped on average 16% every year.

LAF'S TARGET MARKET

LAF's marketing primarily targeted companies that accumulated large volumes of inventory, either because they themselves manufactured the products in large volume or because they served as the middleman in distributing large volumes of manufactured goods from the manufacturers to retailers. These companies often needed to facilitate sales to their own customers using credit products and financial solutions such as short-term loans and leases. LAF was the provider of such financing to over 2,500 such companies nationwide and had a considerable market position, specifically in the home furnishing business and in specialized gift shops. Within these two markets, it was estimated that about one in every five such businesses use LAF's financial solutions in handling their transactions.

While the concentrated focus of LAF in these two markets helped reinforce strong brand loyalty toward the company, it also made the business vulnerable to market downturns. This was very much the case at that time. In recent years, the volume of consumer spending, especially for durable non-essential goods, had dropped significantly due to unique economic and technological forces. Both furniture sales and the gift shop purchases steeply declined as specific consumer segments curbed their non-essential spending and tightened their belts for what looked like rough economic times ahead. This drastic drop in business volume, while shared by most of LAF's national competitors, was a cause for concern at LAF headquarters in Bethesda and for Sanchez, who had to find a way out of this grave scenario.

LAFIN: LIBERTY ASSET FINANCING INVENTORY NEUTRILIZATION

The products that Sanchez was responsible for were marketed under the umbrella name of LAF Inventory Neutralization, or *LAFIN*. LAFIN products consisted of two general families:

Sales Financing (SF): Loans or leases provided to buyers (such as retail chains) to facilitate sales by manufacturers or distributors. Typically LAF's customers who were manufacturers or distributors would promote LAF's Sales Financing products to their own customers in order to speed up the selling process and to increase the probability of a sale.

Inventory Financing (IF): Short-term loans issued to manufacturers or distributors for large volumes of inventory which have built up in their warehouses due to a slowdown in sales. Since these businesses typically have a long history of market presence and warehouses in established locations, issuing short-term loans for such a purpose was generally deemed by LAF as a low-risk business, especially during stable economic times. Manufacturers and distributors often had to rely on such loans in order to manage their short-term cash flow needs and to cover regular business expenses such as payroll costs, utilities, and rent.

Sanchez did not believe that LAF could do much to improve volume in the Sales Financing category. However, she had much higher hopes for Inventory Financing (IF). The slowdown of specific product markets had increased the volume of unsold product inventory in the warehouses of many US-based manufacturers and distributors. Based on industry reports they had studied, Sanchez and her marketing team recognized that the inventory volume of the businesses which they served through IF products had significantly grown over the past year. An industry report indicated that in the past year alone, the volume of inventory by furniture manufacturers that had been stored in a warehouse for more than 6 months had grown by nearly 38%. Sanchez was hoping to capitalize this growth on.

To capitalize on this growth, Sanchez had to reexamine LAFIN's pricing. She believe that while having a dominant position in the specific market of home furnishing and gift shops may have helped LAF during good times, the pressing market conditions had intensified the competition. As result, she and some of her sales managers believed that LAF financial solutions had become overpriced compared to the competition and that the LAF brand name was no longer valued as strongly by customers as it was during better economic times. Customers were now looking for more competitive prices and better value. Therefore, she decided to commission an extensive pricing study.

THE PRICING STUDY

Price Analytics Research Corporation (PARC), an international marketing research firm specializing in optimizing corporate pricing practices, was hired to conduct the study. PARC conducted an extensive survey to assess the level of price sensitivity of customers for Inventory Financing (IF) products. A total of 63 randomly selected operations managers of furniture manufacturers and distributors were recruited for this study. These individuals were identified using publically available information as well as trade and industry association membership lists. The respondents were pre-screened to ensure that they had experience with LAF and three of its major competitors in the past and therefore have the necessary knowledge to accurately respond to the survey questions. Survey administration was conducted online and the respondents were paid $150 for participation.

The pricing of most Inventory Financing (IF) products is driven by two price dimensions. One dimension is the application fee associated with applying for financing. This fee can be waived on rare occasions but in some cases may be as high as $125 per application. LAFIN typically charges an application processing fee of $75. The second pricing dimension is the interest rate associated with the loan. This rate was often based on the 'spread', which is the percentage increment over the prime interest rate. This increment typically ranged from 0.5% to as high as 7.5% over the prime rate, depending on the level of risk LAF associated with the transaction. For example, if at the time of issuing the loan the prime rate is 3%, a spread of 2% would result in an interest rate of 5% being charged. Since the prime rate varies from time to time, the spread was often used as the measure of the price competitiveness of an IF product in terms of interest rates. The combination of the spread and the application fee determines the overall price for inventory financing.

To determine the price competitiveness of LAFIN, a questionnaire consisting of three parts was developed by PARC. The first part of the questionnaire measured the respondent's thresholds to variations in price. The second part of the questionnaire consisted of a conjoint analysis study, whereby the respondent was shown variations of *IF* products and asked to rate each of them. The final part of the questionnaire asked the respondent to rate LAF and three of its major competitors on various price and service quality attributes. The objective of this part of the questionnaire was to develop a visual map which would help Sanchez and her staff to determine the price competitiveness of LAFIN in the IF category. The structure of the questionnaire is outlined below.

Part 1: Price Thresholds

A set of standard questions were used to ascertain what price levels respondents viewed as acceptable. The specific questions asked were:

1. *At what price would you consider this [application fee/spread] to be a good value?*

2. *At what price would you say the [application fee/spread] is beginning to get expensive, but you would still consider moving forward with the transaction?*

Since IF products have two price dimensions, the above set of questions were asked once for the application fee and once for the spread. The exhibit below provides a summary of the results.

	"At what price would you consider this [application fee/spread] to be a good value?"		"At what price would you say the [application fee/spread] is beginning to get expensive, but you would still consider moving forward with the transaction?"	
Application Fee ($)	$0	17 respondents	$0	0 respondent
	$10	11 respondents	$10	3 respondents
	$25	9 respondents	$25	6 respondents
	$50	15 respondents	$50	7 respondents
	$65	7 respondents	$65	16 respondents
	$75	2 respondents	$75	13 respondents
	$100	2 respondents	$100	18 respondents
Spread (%)	0.5%	23 respondents	0.5%	0 respondent
	1.0%	13 respondents	1.0%	2 respondents
	2.5%	16 respondents	2.5%	4 respondents
	5.0%	5 respondents	5.0%	26 respondents
	6.5%	4 respondents	6.5%	16 respondents
	7.5%	1 respondent	7.5%	8 respondents
	10.0%	1 respondent	10.0%	7 respondents

Part 2: Conjoint Analysis

The second part of the questionnaire developed by PARC consisted of a conjoint task. Subjects were told that they would be evaluating a series of Inventory Financing price offers and asked to rate them. The conjoint task systematically varied the two pricing components (application fee and spread). Application fee was varied at four levels: Free, $25, $50, and $75. The spread was also varied at four levels: 0.5%, 2.5%, 5%, and 7.5%. This resulted in sixteen possible combinations (4 levels of application fees × 4 levels of spread).

Each of these combinations was shown to the respondent on a computer screen and at the bottom of the screen the respondent was asked to rate his/her preference for the price presented on a scale of 1 ("not interested at all") to 7 ("extremely interested"). The order of presentation of the various profiles was randomly changed for each respondent in order to avoid any possible order or carryover effects. The summary results for the 63 respondents are provided in exhibit below.

Application Fee \ Spread	0.5%	2.5%	5.0%	7.5%
Free	6.7	6.5	6.3	3.4
$25	6.1	5.8	5.3	2.8
$50	5.9	5.3	2.8	2.4
$75	2.8	2.2	2.3	2.1

Part 3: Rating of LAF and its Competitors

The final section of the questionnaire administered by PARC consisted of a series of questions which measured LAF's Inventory Financing products and comparable products offered by three of its major national competitors. This section of the questionnaire focused on the following measures:

(a) Rating of the prices offered by LAF and its competitors

(b) Rating of the quality of service provided by LAF and its competitors

(c) Importance of various prices and service attributes in general

In addition, the respondents were asked about the importance of price versus quality in their financial decisions. When asked whether a low price or high service quality was important to them, 81% of the respondents chose low price and 19% chose service quality. The summary of this section of the survey is provided in the two exhibits below.

Questions Asked	Importance Weight
IMPORTANCE OF PRICE ATTRIBUTES:	
Importance of having a low application fee	28%
Importance of having a low spread	72%
IMPORTANCE OF SERVICE QUALITY:	
Importance of speedy processing	58%
Importance of personal care by salesperson	42%

	LAFIN	Competitor A	Competitor B	Competitor C
PRICE-RELATED ATTRIBUTES				
Has a low application fee	3.52	5.42	2.91	6.31
Has a low spread	4.23	5.91	3.41	2.35
SERVICE-RELATED ATTRIBUTES				
Speedy processing of the application	6.34	4.52	3.21	5.89
Salesperson exhibits high degree of personal care	5.44	3.82	4.16	6.19

* Note that the names of competitors A, B and C are disguised in order to protect the confidentiality of the survey. The reported figures are averages on 1 to 7 scales with 7 being the positive end of the scale. Market shares for these competitors based on 2009 figures were estimated to be as follows: LAFIN (16%), Competitor A (49%), Competitor B (27%), Competitor C (8%).

THE DECISION FACING SANCHEZ

Having waited over two months for the completion of the pricing study and having incurred a consulting fee nearing $50,000, Sanchez had to determine if LAFIN products are properly positioned in the marketplace. The first quarter of the current year was about to come to a close. With the time pressure put on her by the Board of Directors, the challenging market conditions of the time, and the notable drop in LAF's business the previous year, pricing of LAFIN was of central concern.

CASE QUESTION

Based on the presented research, what do you believe should be the price of LAFIN, in terms of the application fee and the spread?

LEXZMMAR INVESTMENTS

COMPANY BACKGROUND

Located in Seattle, WA, Lexzmmar Investments is a fund management firm which has managed an array of successful mutual funds for nearly eight decades. Founded by Joseph Lexzmmar in 1933, the company's investment products have traditionally been among the most innovative in the industry. Lexzmmar was a Finnish immigrant who came to the U.S. in 1927 to complete a Ph.D. in economics. While completing his Ph.D., he managed to publish several scientific articles that have since become classics in economic theory and finance. Upon the completion of his Ph.D. in 1931, he was offered several top academic positions in leading universities in the U.S. and Europe. However, Joseph Lexzmmar always had a preference for practicality that manifested itself in a passionate interest in the complexities of everyday investment decisions rather than the theoretical abstractions of academic work. As a result, he joined one of the leading banks on the West Coast as an economist upon graduation. He rose quickly through the ranks and was promoted to the status of Chief Investment Officer within five years.

In the early 1930s, the banking sector in the U.S. experienced considerable turmoil. Due to the inadequate banking regulations, many banks had actively engaged their customers' deposits in high-risk investments; the Great Depression caused great fear and a majority of consumers withdrew their funds from the banks. With poor investment returns and without sufficient deposits in their vaults, many banks began to collapse and a series of catastrophic bank failures followed. These failures resulted in a state of economic turmoil, increased regulations, and the elimination of many management positions within the banking sector. Soon, people like Joseph Lexzmmar found themselves unemployed in a distressed and unstable industry. In 1935, having been relieved of his duties by his former employer, Joseph Lexzmmar set out to establish his own investment company. Lexzmmar believed that many individuals like himself were wrongfully deprived of their professional lives due to an industry's poor management style and failing regulations.

MANAGEMENT PHILOSOPHY

In 1935, Joseph Lexzmmar set out on a mission to build a company where he could combine his visions of investment strategy with scientific models of financial markets. This combination would produce innovative financial products that could help the masses. One of the guiding principles in Lexzmmar's management style was the central importance of the client. He made a point of spending at least one third of his own time with clients of all wealth levels. Lexzmmar's hands-on style was unique; despite being one of the wealthiest bankers on the West Coast, he typically logged nearly one thousand hours of one-on-one time with Lexzmmar clients every year.

One of the other guiding principles that Joseph Lexzmmar established in his company was the importance of innovation. He believed that clients often appreciate products that resolve their investment constraints, and he encouraged his managers to spend considerable time sharing their observations with one another in order to understand clients' needs. He believed this to be a fruitful way to design and develop new investment products. The result of this approach to innovation was the introduction of new breeds of mutual funds. These were highly attractive not only to Lexzmmar's own clients but also to competing fund companies, many of whom eventually became distributors of some of Lexzmmar's investment products for their own client base. In a 1941 interview with a financial reporter, Joseph Lexzmmar was quoted as saying, "customers are the lifeblood of this business ... we need to listen to them to see what we should do tomorrow ... without them there would be no tomorrow for us."

This approach to business resulted in consistent and impressive growth. Between 1935 and 1940, the number of clients grew from 50 to well over 500. The total assets under management grew from $2.1 million to $130 million. One of the contributing factors of this growth was the unique approach used to compensate Lexzmmar employees. Nearly half of the salaries of employees with client contact (for example, investment professionals, customer service employees, and fund managers) were linked to the financial performance of the client portfolios and the results of client satisfaction surveys. This approach was considered revolutionary at that time, as the typical broker's compensation was based on the number of securities trades made by clients; brokers in competing firms were rarely held accountable for clients' account performance or client satisfaction. In 1957, the explosive growth of the client base led the company to impose a stop-growth policy limiting new account issuance. This decision was based on Joseph Lexzmmar's driving principle of maintaining high levels of customer care and individualized attention. However, to support growth, Lexzmmar gradually developed a branch infrastructure and expanded its workforce; at the time of this case study the company had nearly 11,000 clients and operated 17 branch offices in eight major cities in the states of Washington, California, and Arizona.

Many of the company's mutual fund products are sold today through other fund companies, brokers, advisors, and even a select group of commercial banks.

PERFORMANCE PROTECTED PRODUCTS

Joseph Lexzmmar's approach to running a successful investment business remained with the company after his passing. Randall Weinstein was hired as the company's CEO. Weinstein, 48, had a long history of running several successful investment banks in New York and was a well-respected individual in the industry, having authored numerous landmark business articles and two best-selling books on investment strategy. His business philosophy and credentials, which in many ways resembled those of the company's founder, were the primary reasons he was hired for the job. Nevertheless, Weinstein was challenged by many forces. The poor performance of the stock market in the recent past had made many Lexzmmar clients unhappy with their investment results. Furthermore, the competitive environment of fund management companies was quickly changing. The emergence of mobile banking, mobile payments, online trading, the aggressive pursuit of the market by discount brokers, and the unease caused by uncertainty about interest rates vastly complicated the decisions that Weinstein would have to make.

One of the decisions facing Weinstein at that time was the possible launch of what the company's investment strategists had named Performance Protected Products (PPPs). These short-term investment products provide market-linked returns such as stock market indexed mutual funds which follow the general trends in particular stock markets. They protect investors from potential downturns in investment value. When a client purchases a PPP, she agrees to invest in the product and not to withdraw the invested amounts for a pre-specified period of time. At the end of the time-period, the investor is then able to collect the originally deposited funds plus any applicable investment returns. The attractive characteristic of the PPP was that Lexzmmar would guarantee the product against downward movement in asset value upon maturity. Therefore, the originally invested amount would be protected, and clients' potential investment losses would be eliminated if the market were to go down. The eventual investment returns of PPPs were linked to the returns on the major exchanges and established stock indexes.

Lexzmmar investment strategists had developed three versions of PPPs: one linked to the S&P 500 Index, the other linked to the NASDAQ, and the last linked to the Toronto Stock Exchange (TSE). It was believed that these investment products would attract investors since they allowed active participation in some of the major investment markets while providing protection against downward drops in investment value. To participate in PPPs, clients were charged 2.5% of the total investment amount on a yearly basis. Weinstein, however, believed that, while the 2.5% upfront cost may detract some clients from investing, levels as high as 5% to 10% might be needed to provide some "insurance" against possible downward trends in the stock market. Given the poor stock market results in recent years, this became a central question for the product team.

Despite his reservations, Weinstein's discussions with the PPP product team and his understanding of the company's guiding principles suggested to him that this product fit many of Joseph Lexzmmar's guiding principles. PPPs provided Lexzmmar's existing clients with a broader range of investment choices. The product was innovative and would enable these clients to remain active in the stock market even in volatile times. Furthermore, PPPs provided other brokers, investment advisors, and third parties the ability to introduce their own customers to a new approach to investing in the stock market while limiting any downward movements in investment value.

MARKET RESEARCH

Having only been at Lexzmmar for less than a month, Weinstein was hesitant to undertake any major product launches without some form of scientific market research.

To help understand clients' possible responses to Performance Protected Products, Weinstein asked the PPP product team to commission a market research study designed to determine the product's optimal marketing strategy. Several marketing issues were to be investigated. The first was the effects of the upfront costs on client interest. The second concern was the receptiveness of the clients to direct mail information about the product. These two factors constituted the primary marketing tools available to Lexzmmar at that time to market PPPs to the client base.

The market research firm designed a systematic experiment in which different groups of clients received product brochures by mail. Subsequently, the number of inquiries generated were tabulated and quantified. The experiment engaged a total of 900 clients who were split into six equally sized groups of 150 clients. Each group was mailed direct mail pieces with detailed descriptions of the PPP products, including the upfront investment fees. The number of direct mail pieces sent to each group varied from two to six (in increments of two), and the upfront fees varied at two levels: 2.5% and 5%. The number of customer inquiries was tracked by recording the tracking number included in the direct mail brochures sent out to each customer from those clients who called Lexzmmar's Client Care line to request additional information. The direct mail brochures were sent out and the exhibit below summarizes the results. The reported response rates in the exhibit were measured by counting the number of clients who responded to the direct mail pieces, making a follow-up inquiry, and requesting additional product information within fifteen days of the mailing. It was expected that one in every ten clients who respond to the brochure would eventually purchase a PPP product from Lexzmmar.

Number of Direct Mail Pieces Sent Out	Upfront Fee at 2.5%	Upfront Fee at 5%
2	11 out of 150 clients contacted	6 out of 150 clients contacted
4	21 out of 150 clients contacted	9 out of 150 clients contacted
6	35 out of 150 clients contacted	11 out of 150 clients contacted

It was estimated that the cost of a single mailing is $1.50. Furthermore, the incremental yearly administrative costs of launching PPP products and servicing the client base were estimated at $450,000. Furthermore, using statistical models and several financial assumptions, the product team estimated that one in ten clients to whom the product is promoted would purchase it. The incremental life-time profit estimates associated with clients who were pitched PPP products at the 2.5% and 5% fee levels were produced by the Finance department at Lexzmmar and are provided in the exhibit below. The exhibit shows the expected incremental profit figures, based on data from those customers who had purchased PPP products in the market experiment. The shown figures represent the incremental life-time profits expected from the client due to the purchase of the PPP product, developed based on a financial model used by Lexzmmar analysts.

Number of Direct Mail Pieces Sent	Upfront Fee at 2.5%	Upfront Fee at 5%
2	$4,124	$6,394
4	$4,359	$6,596
6	$4,284	$3,897

CASE QUESTIONS

1. What is the optimal launch strategy for Lexzmmar's Performance Protected Products?

2. Develop a marketing plan including a chronology of activities that Lexzmmar should undertake during the first 3 years of product introduction.

TIRE INSURANCE PROGRAM

Norvest Banc, located in Seattle Washington, was a strong regional competitor, providing a variety of financial solutions in the states of Washington, Oregon, Montana and Idaho. Established in 1962, Norvest provided this market with a range of credit and insurance products for both individual and business customers and operated over 130 bank branches in the four states. At the time of this case, due to the changing economic climate, the potential for growth for institutions such as Norvest seemed somewhat limited. Consumer spending was on a decline, the housing market was experiencing price drops, and access to credit was limited due to increased lender sensitivity to risk.

The collapse of the mortgage-backed securities market had further made the business climate unfavorable for lending institutions, and new regulatory measures were being implemented to enforce higher standards for lending practices. In this environment, consumers' sense of insecurity about their financial future encouraged them to save more, thereby increasing their savings deposits. However, consumers no longer took out the volume of loans they did in years earlier. As a result, products such as home equity loans, lines of credit, and mortgages witnessed historic drops in application volume and issuance rates, both for Norvest and its competitors. The low interest environment of the time further limited Norvest Banc's profits, so the management primarily focused on drastic measures to pursue profit growth.

THE NORVEST BANC MISSION

Norvest Banc's CEO, John Dawes, along with the Chief Marketing Office, Nancy Hawthorne, had discussed the need for a niche-driven approach to growth in this challenging environment. Discussing this potential in the annual meeting with branch managers, Dawes had pointed out that *"the traditional markets we serve are bound to shrink next year and the only way to sustain our current size is to find untapped pockets of potential."* He then charged Hawthorne with the task of finding these pockets and to initiate actions that will help Norvest to capitalize on them.

Hawthorne's task was a challenging one. As a former technology specialist for a major software developer, she appreciated the need for embracing change and realigning the organization to capitalize on new opportunities. The pressures of the environment and the demands of senior management required quick and successful execution of creative marketing campaigns for innovative products. Hawthorne was most conerned that many failing banks and their branch operations would be acquired by larger competitors, increasing the power of the few national players in Norvest's regional markets and inhibiting the bank's ability to compete based on its recognized brand name and its efficient cost structure. Recent trends of bank mergers and acquisitions both at the national and regional levels indicated that they generate cost efficiencies and produce new organizations that can take over the market more aggressively. This was a story which she was very familiar with in her previous career in the software industry and did not want to see repeated in the case of Norvest.

GROWTH OPPORTUNITIES

Unlike the bigger national banks with great resources, Novest Banc could not expand of its retail presence by opening or acquiring new branches because of its financial constraints. However, Hawthorne and Dawes began discussing specific steps Norvest could take in order to combat the evident market pressures. Some of the ideas that emerged from these discussions soon evolved into specific marketing campaigns and products which could be launched within a very short time period. For example, more aggressive marketing campaigns were deployed to promote the bank's credit card products to existing customers. Also, short-term credit products began to be systematically promoted to business customers by the bank branches' loan officers. Some of these steps were dramatic shifts in Norvest's marketing philosophy. For example, traditionally Norvest did not promote credit card products to its existing customers since Dawes previously believed that credit card marketing is a mass-market operation and should not be undertaken by regional banks. Now, Norvest recognized the need to push this product line even if they were late in the game, especially compared to many of its local competitors. They executed more aggressive promotion programs by directly mailing existing customers. This included promotional material in monthly bank statements as well as more visible advertising for various credit card options available to online banking customers on the bank's web site.

A second initiative that developed from the conversations between Dawes and Hawthorne was the expansion of the number of Automatic Teller Machines (ATMs) operated by Norvest. The goal was to identify strategic locations that have little presence of competing ATM machines but experience high volumes of pedestrian traffic. A total of 68 locations in the four states were identified, and ATM machines were leased and installed in these locations. The ATM fees generated from these machines were projected to create a profitable return, with a projected ROI of approximately 16%.

The third initiative discussed between Hawthorne and Dawes was to expand the company's insurance business into very specialized categories of insurance. The deregulation of the financial services industry had long made this a possibility for banking institutions such as Norvest. The repeal of the Glass-Steagall Act made it possible for financial institutions to become active in a wide range of financial markets. This opened new opportunities for banks to become active participants in the insurance business – a potential that only a limited number of banking institutions effectively capitalized on.

THE TIRE INSURANCE PROGRAM (TIP)

The inspiration behind Hawthorne's insurance product came out of a minor driving incident she experienced the previous summer. While driving on one of the major highways north of Seattle, her car ran over debris that had fallen from a construction truck ahead. She momentarily lost control of the vehicle but managed to avoid collision with other vehicles and successfully slowed her vehicle down to a stop. When she stepped out of her car she realized that one of the front tires had been punctured by a sharp piece of metal, beyond the point of repair. Being an avid sports car driver she knew that to replace this high-performance tire she would be spending nearly $350, and her automobile insurance policy did not cover such expenses.

This incident sparked Hawthorne's interest in developing an insurance product for Norvest Banc called TIP. TIP, which stands for "Tire Insurance Program", would consist of tire insurance coverage to protect car owners when facing situations similar to what Hawthorne had experienced. If the tire becomes damaged for any reason beyond the point of a simple repair, TIP would pay the full replacement cost of the tire, including installation costs. Such products are widely promoted by national chains of tire distributors. However, Hawthorne's market research revealed that the majority of independent service stations and repair shops, while accounting for over 30% of all tires sold in the country, do not offer such a product to their customers. To Hawthorne, this represented the "pockets of potential" that Dawes had tasked her to look for. In addition, such incidents were often not covered by automobile insurance companies since the associated costs fell below the typical deductible level of $500 associated with auto insurance policies.

TIP could therefore represent a good option for many car owners and service stations that may benefit from promoting it to their customers. Market research indicated that tires on most vehicles last about 38,000 miles, allowing for a driving period of 32 months. Replacement costs for all four tires vary from car to car and depend on the tire size and performance characteristics. Tire size (e.g., "225/50/16") is quantified by three measures : (a) the width of the tire (e.g., 225 millimeters), (b) side wall aspect ratio representing the size of the sidewall height compared to the radius of the tire (e.g., 50 would mean 50%), and (c) the wheel diameter in inches (e.g., 16 inches). In addition, factors such as the speed rating of the tire (how fast the vehicle could be driven), the weight rating (what load the tire could carry) and the material used to construct the tire affected its value to buyers. The exhibit below provides a sampling of tire prices. Market research by industry associations and expert estimates indicated significant variation in replacement costs ranging from a low of about $250 for four tires to a high of over $2,000 for high performance tires.

Tire Size	Replacement Cost
195/65/15	$60-$115
205/60/16	$75-$125
215/60/16	$80-$125
215/65/17	$95-$155
225/65/17	$120-$180
235/55/18	$110-$210
245/65/17	$115-$395
275/65/18	$135-$525

However, research also indicated that the primary cause of tire replacement is the natural wear and tear on the tire, poor wheel alignment, or faulty suspension systems on the vehicle. Tire punctures due to nails resulting in tire deflation were often easily repaired at an average cost of $23, and catastrophic tire failures due to large objects – like the one experienced by Hawthorne resulting in the need for total replacement of the tire – were very rare. Less than half of one percent of all tires replaced were assumed to be due to such catastrophic failures. However, consumers tend to overestimate the likelihood of such events, and given the high price for replacing the tire often opt to purchase the additional tire protection polices from chains of tire retailers that offer them. This represents a great profit opportunity for these retailers and insurers who underwrite the policies. Similar patterns had been observed in home electronics retailing, whereby major retail chains were able to reap unprecedented profits by selling supplemental warranties for major appliances and electronic products. While these warranties provided customers with peace of mind, the low incident of product failures during the term of the coverage transformed extended warranties to a source of profits which at times exceeded the profit margins for the majority of electronic products sold by these retailers. Hawthorne wondered if the same profit opportunity may await Norvest if TIP were to be launched.

DISTRIBUTION SYSTEM FOR AUTOMOBILE TIRES

Tire protection policies had been sold for well over a decade by national and regional chains of tire retailers. While tires can be expensive and tend to account for a large portion of the cost of maintaining a vehicle, the increased level of competition over the years reduced the ability of tire retailers to realize high margins on the sale of tires alone. Price competition and the publicizing and advertising of prices have become common practice in this business, creating downward pressure on prices. In order to counter the resulting margin depletion, tire retailers have developed new approaches to generate profits. Often the advertised prices do not include the cost of installation, nor are the costs of disposal of the old tires explicitly mentioned in the ads. While consumers may be drawn to a particular retailer due to its low advertised price for the tire, they may not pay sufficient attention to these additional costs. These costs represent lucrative sources of profits for the retailer, especially when a large volume of tires is sold.

An additional source of profits for chains of tire retailers has been supplemental tire protection policies, which represent little costs and can significantly boost the profits associated with the individual sale of tires. When pitched effectively to customers who are about to spend hundreds of dollars replacing their old tires, tire protection policies represent a small fraction of the overall expenditure, yet they create a sense of security in the customer's mind and as a result, many customers accept. Some estimated that about 21% of all tires sold by those retailers that offer them were sold in conjunction with such a policy. However, the infrequent occurrence of catastrophic tire failures made the costs of providing such insurance protection very low, and while a supplemental coverage for a single tire may cost the customer as much as $15 per tire, the cost of providing such coverage could be less than 50¢ to the insurer.

Hawthorne's desire to launch TIP aligned with the general direction that Norvest Banc had taken in advancing its position in the insurance markets in its region. A central part of Norvest's marketing strategy was to establish itself in insurance markets that experienced low incident rates for policyholder claims yet were experiencing stable growth in policy sales. Tire protection certainly fit these two criteria and, following discussions with Dawes and the legal team at Norvest, Hawthorne sought and obtained regulatory permission to launch TIP. Hawthorne, recognizing that the national and regional chains of tire retailers already have tire replacement programs in place, decided not to approach them and to instead focus Norvest's efforts on independent service stations. These service stations often consist of a gas station which may carry fuel from major oil companies, a convenience store, and a repair shop. Due to their independent nature, the tires sold by these stations to their customers are often not pitched to customers with the added option of tire protection – a feature heavily promoted by competing chains of tire retailers.

The independent service stations are often family-operated businesses and provide repair service to the population in the immediate vicinity of the station. As a result, they tend to be stable businesses that have long-established customer relationships, and many of the station operators have had bank accounts or other financial transactions with Norvest bank branches located near them. This, Hawthorne believed, created the pocket of opportunity: "We know these folks, and they know us, and the trust they have in us can make this venture work, as long as we put enough resources behind it and price TIP properly." She estimated that in the four states where Norvest has bank branches, there are over 3,600 service stations that can be pitched with TIP.

TESTING THE WATERS

In order to test the waters, Hawthorne decided to launch the product concept in Idaho first. If the Idaho results turn out to be favorable, she would then launch TIP in the other three states. The Idaho launch would also enable her to examine the market acceptance rate and degree of price sensitivity associated with TIP. As a result, TIP each Norvest bank branch in Idaho was asked to assign one staff member to approach a target group of service stations in its immediate vicinity. The use of existing bank staff for this incremental effort was partially motivated by Hawthorne's view that existing employees should be retained as much as possible despite the slowdown in business, and reallocation of some employees to new marketing activities would help prevent the need for employee layoffs. To further motivate branch staff assigned with this task, a $50 commission for every service station that signs up with TIP would be paid to the employee.

To enable a flexible selling process, the employee would be able to set the retail price of TIP (price paid by the customer to the service station) anywhere between $5 a tire to $15 per tire. Furthermore, the salesperson would be able to vary the retail margins from 40% to 75%. For example, having set the retail price at $10 and a 40% margin, the customer would pay $10 per tire to obtain the protection by TIP, and the service station would pass on $6 to Norvest Banc and keep the remaining $4. The exact terms would be negotiated between the bank employee and each service station operator and could therefore vary from one service station to the next. The cost of underwriting TIP to Norvest, as reflected by the actuarial cost of replacing a damaged tire, was estimated to be 54¢ (this cost takes into account both the probability of catastrophic tire failure and the replacement cost of the tire). This figure ranged from a low of 37¢ for smaller tires to a high of $3.45 for high-performance tires.

The Norvest marketing group internally debated whether the prices should be tiered so that coverage for the more expensive high-performance tires would be priced at higher levels. However, Dawes believed in launching a simple pricing scheme and ideally a universal program that could be implemented in an identical form across all states. No agreement on a tiered price structure was reached by the January launch date in Idaho. It was therefore decided to launch the product in Idaho at a single price regardless of tire size and type. This decision was made considering that the industry norm – as exercised by the chain tire retailers – was to charge a single price for all sizes and types of tires being protected by the policy. However, to allow some flexibility in the selling process, the bank staff making the pitch to the service station operators could offer the operators a gift card valued anywhere between $10 to $25. To prevent cases of abuse, half of the value of this card would be funded from the $50 commission paid to the employee. Therefore, if a service station signs up for TIP and is offered a $10 gift card, the bank employee would only receive $45 (i.e., $50 less $10×½).

The selling of TIP was a relatively systematic process. Each Norvest bank branch manager received a list of service stations in the branch's surrounding area and was asked to assign one branch employee to visit these stations. In order to ensure a proper sales approach, the selected employee would have to have had previous selling experience and would conduct background checks on the list of service stations provided by the Norvest head office in order to prioritize selling efforts on the larger and more established businesses. About 19% of businesses were eliminated from further processing either due to their unfavorable financial standing or questionable status as judged by the bank branch manager. The remaining 81% of service stations on the list were then approached for the pitch through a personal visit by the bank employee.

Three main selling points were emphasized in such visits. One was the established brand name of Norvest Banc in the neighborhood, which would make it easy for the service station to pitch the product to its customers. The second benefit pitched was the ability of the service station to introduce a new benefit to its customers, and the third benefit – perhaps the most important – was the incremental profits that the service station could realize from promoting TIP to those customers who buy tires. These visits resulted in a success rate of 22%, with the service station operator signing up to offer TIP to its customers during the sales visit. Follow-up calls to the service station operator boosted this success rate to 37%. Of the 238 service stations approached over the three months following the launch, a total of 88 service stations signed up for TIP. To enable tracking, the service station was required through the signed agreement to disclose the total number of tires it sells every month, regardless of whether or not TIP was sold alongside the tire. This would enable Norvest head office analysts to examine TIP's market penetration and observe the potential effects of its pricing and promotion campaigns.

DATA FROM THE IDAHO LAUNCH

The 238 stations approached during the 3-month test market period represented 31% of all service stations registered in the five-mile radius of the Norvest branches in Idaho. To document the effectiveness of the selling process, data from the bank employees was consolidated. The resulting data set captured the characteristics of each individual sales visit, including information on the TIP price pitched by the employee, the value of the gift card offered (if any), the retail margin pitched, and whether or not the retailer signed for TIP. The exhibit below provides a summary of the sales information.

Number of tires sold per station	27.6
Number of tires sold with TIP per station	8.1
Retail price of TIP	$9.39
Retail margin	54.90%
Value of gift card given to the service station	$9.56

HAWTHORNE'S CHALLENGE

Given the results of the Idaho launch, Nancy Hawthorne needed to consider the expansion of TIP to Oregon, Montana and Washington, in addition to further penetration of the Idaho market. In her assessment the cost of the staff reaching out to service station operators was already captured by each bank branch's infrastructure expenses and did not represent incremental expenses to Norvest. This assessment was a reflection of the direction given by the Board of Directors of Norvest to mobilize underutilized bank staff for such projects. However, many other issues remained to be assessed regarding pricing and promotion campaigns. Specifically, Hawthorne had been asked by Dawes and the Board to develop a universal marketing program based on the Idaho experience. Dawes had suggested to her that keeping the price and promotion (e.g., gift cards) flexible can make the program very difficult to manage and cause considerable confusion among customers and branch employees. It also introduces potential sources of tension if service station operators and their customers from neighboring areas realize that they have been offered different prices for the exact same coverage levels, and can therefore potentially compromise their trust and confidence in Norvest – something that Dawes wanted to avoid given the sense of public distrust that had developed toward the financial services sector at that time.

Hawthorne was therefore charged with the task of determining the optimal price and promotion program for TIP based on the data collected from Idaho. The base program being considered offered a TIP price per tire of $10, a $10 gift card to the station operators and a 50% retail margin. These figures closely resembled the numbers which evolved out of Idaho. Additionally, Hawthorne had to evaluate four other options:

(A)   The same program as the base program being considered, however at a TIP price per tire of $5 (i.e., price: $5, gift card: $10, retail margin: 50%).

(B)   The same program as the base program being considered, however at a TIP price per tire of $15 (i.e., price: $15, gift card: $10, retail margin: 50%).

(C)   The same program as the base program (TIP price per tire of $10 and 50% retail margin), however without any gift cards being given to the service stations (i.e., price: $10, gift card: $0, retail margin: 50%).

(D)   The same program as the base program, however with the retail margin boosted to 75% (i.e., price: $10, gift card: $10, retail margin: 75%).

Dawes believed that option D would be the best since it provides a great incentive for the station operators to adopt TIP. However, he also recognized that many of the station operators making decisions on such matters may not have long-term perspective on such decisions and may not consider the retail margin heavily in their decisions. Perhaps for this reason and ethical concerns, he favored option C as well. Dawes viewed the gift card a form of bribe which the station operators may be offended to accept. Given the abundance of data collected from the Idaho test, interpretations of such type no longer needed to be a matter of personal opinions; Hawthorne and her staff could settle the issue through scientific analysis.

CASE QUESTION

What is the optimal price for launching TIP?

GEORGIA SUPPLEMENTAL

Georgia Supplemental Insurance (GSI) was a regional provider of supplemental insurance policies in the states of Georgia, South Carolina, and North Carolina. The company prided itself on offering the best value to its customers through supplemental policies for dental, vision, and travel coverage. Georgia (short for Georgia Supplemental Insurance) sold its policies primarily through employers in these three states. Employers in turn promoted the policies to their employees, who could choose to participate in the offered supplemental insurance plans. Employee participation was typically voluntary and associated with regular monthly premiums, which would be paid directly to Georgia by the employee. Employers who chose to make Georgia's policies available to their employees profited from the ability to bring additional benefits to their workers without having to pay for these added benefits themselves.

Georgia Supplemental was founded in 1973 by Samuel Adler. Adler, who at that time was a dental technician with several years of experience, had noted that the majority of his dental patients had little or no dental insurance coverage. He recognized that, while many of the better employers offered health insurance to their workers, dental coverage was rarely a standard part of their benefits package. After being laid off in early 1973, he invested his life savings into building a company that would explore this need. The company was incorporated by the end of that year, and a small office was set up in Atlanta. Georgia's mission was to become a leading provider of supplemental dental insurance coverage for employers in the state of Georgia. In 1975, the company expanded its operations into South Carolina; in 1980, Georgia was pitched offerings to employers in North Carolina. By 1987, the company had expanded its product array to include supplemental vision; in 1993, travel insurance was also added to its offerings.

Traditionally, Georgia had focused on employers with 50 to 250 employees. Adler believed that companies with smaller operations are often financially strapped and may not be able to convince their workers about the benefits of obtaining supplemental insurance. In addition, it was believed that larger insurance companies that provide group medical plans often penetrate the market for companies that have 250 or more employees either through their own products or through partnerships with third parties. Past experience also seemed to suggest that the most receptive group to Georgia's sales pitches were typically employing anywhere between 50 to 250 employees.

Adler was faced with a potentially costly decision to expand Georgia's geographic range while opening up new channels of profitability for the company. Adler had set a personal goal for himself and for Georgia to expand its operations into Florida, where he believed great profit potential existed. Though more promising, the decision to move into Florida may prove to be costlier than any of the other expansions that the company had undertaken in its three-decade history.

THE SELLING OF SUPPLEMENTAL INSURANCE

In the insurance business, most policies have exclusion terms and conditions that limit the amount of benefits for the policyholder. The existence of these exclusions creates a demand for increased coverage either by paying higher premiums to the insurance company or by purchasing supplemental insurance. Supplemental insurance coverage provides benefits that traditional insurance policies may not provide in a cost-effective manner. For example, while a health insurance plan offered by an employer may cover the majority of the costs of a medical procedure, not all costs are covered, which can leave policyholders with medical debts even after paying insurance for years. These policies, for example, do not cover any yearly deductibles or co-pays for which the policyholder is responsible. Furthermore, indirect costs related to medical treatment, such as the cost of lost wages due to missing work or out of pocket expenses such as the cost of transportation to a medical facility, are typically not covered by employee-sponsored health plans. Supplemental health insurance could provide coverage for some of these additional items. Similarly, supplemental dental insurance may cover portions of dental bills and supplemental vision plans may cover some of the costs of eye exams and eyewear for individuals who may not have coverage through their employers. Supplemental insurance plans therefore offer a potentially attractive way to control these common expenditures. In addition to the financial protection that supplemental insurance policies provide to policyholders, they also present attractive profit opportunities to the insurance companies selling them. Adler estimated that the average contribution margin for each individual enrolled in a supplemental health plan is $108. For a supplemental dental plan, the estimated margin was $65 and for supplemental travel and vision, it was estimated to be $37 and $45 respectively for each insured individual.

Supplemental policies can be directly purchased by individuals from an insurance company or its agents; they may also be purchased through employers who make them available to their workers. Georgia Supplemental primarily sold its policies through employers. Before the growing use of the Internet, the company did not have the infrastructure necessary to sell directly to consumers, and it never functioned through an agent organization. Georgia's sales staff personally made sales calls to the human resources administrators or benefits officers at major employers' headquarters. The sales process often consisted of presenting these individuals with a background of the company and its insurance programs, discussing relevant questions, and presenting the various plans and associated prices. Adler estimated that, out of every twenty sales calls or visits made to new prospects, at least one employer would choose to sign up with Georgia. The sales force also revisited existing accounts two to three times a year to secure repeated business and to pitch new products and plans. On a weekly basis, the average salesperson was on the road about four days of the week, making a total of 28 sales visits. Because of these demanding tasks, the sales force was well compensated, and the average salary (base, commissions, and bonuses) for Georgia's 21 sales people was $94,750. Adler estimated that an additional $45,000 had to be spent on transportation and benefits for each sales person.

EXPANSION PLANS

The current sales force covered the states of Georgia and the Carolinas, and over the years these states had helped the company develop 720 loyal accounts (employers), through which 93,560 individual policyholders had obtained supplemental insurance policies from Georgia. The expansion into Florida seemed inevitable to Adler, who often cited state and national statistics to support his long-held beliefs. By his estimates, moving into Florida could double the size of the business in less than five years. Several features of the state were deemed attractive. He also believed that human resources administrators and benefits officers in the state of Florida would be more receptive to Georgia Supplemental and its products. This was based on his own interactions with these individuals in a benefits conference held in Tampa and through informal discussions with his own sales staff. He was also motivated for personal reasons, as Florida was his native state.

A primary source of opportunity was the demographics of Florida, which were quickly changing. While there was a significant population of retired individuals who had moved into Florida to retire, there was also an influx of young families. These families found the low cost of housing, the warmer climate, and good employment opportunities in Florida attractive. This younger market segment formed the basis for Adler's interest in expanding into Florida. He estimated the size of this segment of the population to grow by an average of 6-7% annually over the next decade. The need that these families had for supplemental insurance coverage combined with the promising economic picture of the state made Florida a natural point for expansion.

What further sparked Adler's interest was the limited amount of coverage that employers in Florida typically offered with their standard employee benefit plans. A survey conducted the previous year by Benefits Research Inc (BRI) showed that the average family had to spend $480 out of pocket to cover dental expenses, of which only $139 was for preventive care. BRI also found that, in Florida, only 17% of employers provided vision coverage as part of their standard health plans, whereas nearly half of the population needed some form of vision care every year. The survey also found that most employers did not participate in travel insurance programs, and that only 6% of employers offered some form of travel insurance policy to their workers. BRI estimated that the total potential market in Florida that would meet Georgia Supplemental's criteria is 3,580 employers, with a total of about half a million employees, each of whom may have several family members in need of supplemental policies.

ADLER'S DECISION

Adler would have to soon arrive at his decision. The strategy to move into Florida could prove to be a costly one. Adler has devised a plan to lead a newly hired sales force into Florida by first sending personalized direct mail letters to the human resources managers in the 3,580 companies identified by BRI (exhibit on the next page), costing the company nearly $75,000 (production, mailing, list acquisition). The mailing would be conducted by Georgia's marketing department in Atlanta and would be followed up with sales calls and visits by a newly formed Florida sales force that would be in full force by the following year. The yearly overhead cost of setting up a branch office in Tampa was estimated at about $250,000. For a CEO who had been at the helm for over three decades, and for a company that had not launched into a new market for over a decade, this could prove to be a more challenging decision than anyone had originally expected.

CASE QUESTIONS

1. Should Georgia launch into Florida?

2. What is your assessment of the proposed direct mail campaign and the promotional letter?

James Winterz
Georgia Supplemental Insurance
391 Brook Street, Suite 9A
Tampa, FL

Wilfred Lampelle
Human Resources Manager
APCO Electronics
Miami, FL

Dear Mr. Lampelle,

Please allow me to introduce my company, Georgia Supplemental Insurance (GSI) and myself. GSI is a provider of supplemental insurance policies to employers throughout Florida, Georgia, and the Carolinas. We have been in business for over three decades and provide supplemental health insurance to nearly 100,000 happy employees. GSI provides companies like yours with the ability to provide an array of attractive supplemental insurance policies, from which your employees are very likely to benefit. Our dental plan provides employees and their families with two yearly exams and a 75% discount on major dental procedures[1]. Our vision plan provides a yearly exam for all family members and a 50% discount on eyewear1. We also provide a travel insurance plan and will soon be providing our policyholders with a supplemental health plan[2].

Customer satisfaction and quality service to our policyholders is a founding belief at GSI. We believe that our generous treatment of the customer and liberal and quick processing of claims is the driving force behind why so many companies like yours have chosen to provide our services to their employees.

In the next few weeks, I will be contacting you to see if it is possible to meet briefly and discuss together the details of GSI's plans, which I believe will be very beneficial to APCCO employees. In the meantime, please do not hesitate to call me or my secretary Robert Gains at (217)xxx-xxxx. I look forward to speaking with you shortly.

Sincerely,

James Winterz
Sales Manager
Georgia Supplemental Insurance

---

1. At participating dental offices
2. Subject to state approval

PHOENIX CARDS INC. (PCI)

On a hot summer day in July, a heated discussion between the Chief Marketing Officer (CMO) and the head of the Human Resources (HR) department of Phoenix Cards could be heard outside the CMO's office. These were difficult and definitional times for PCI – a company that had for many years successfully grown in the business of supplying gift cards and prepaid debit cards to thousands of retailers around the country. From what could be gathered from the loud and sometimes muffled conversations, the CMO – John Hawking – had asked Randy Xavier, the head of HR to come to his office for an urgent discussion. The discussion had to do with Hawking's need for an explanation as to why the hiring of 34 sales people had been turned down by the HR department. One could hear Hawking screaming: *"The growth is inevitable and you are stalling the company."*

Hawking was a 9-year veteran in the sales and marketing field. He had started his career right out of college, selling used cars through a major national chain of used car dealerships, focusing on online sales. After 2 years in that position, he ran for local public office and served for 3 years as an elected public official. He then joined a national financial services firm, first as a financial advisor and then as a marketing manager. He had joined PCI just two years ago as the Chief Marketing Officer. Hawking believes that growth is the only path for PCI and that all barriers to the company's growth need to be eliminated: *"We are in a commoditized business, and failure to innovate would translate to obsolescence"*. His argument did not sit well with Xavier, who also had many years of work experience. He had started his career out of college as an accountant working for a European-based corporation. After 3 years in that position, he moved to an accounting firm in Los Angeles, where he began as a junior accountant in the audit division, and eventually moved up to regional manager of all of the firm' audit activities for the West Coast. After 4 years in that position he made a career shift, moving to PCI as a manager in the HR department, and eventually after 2 years as the head of the HR department.

The two men not only held contrasting views on business but also had very different personalities. Xavier's gentle, introverted and reserved manners stood in clear contrast to Hawking's outgoing and extroverted manners. This was evident as Hawking abruptly slammed the door to his office to block out the small number of employees who had gathered right outside, curious about the commotion. From thereon, all that could be heard was the loud back-and-forth shouting, often mumbled by the sound of the rush-hour evening traffic passing by on the highway right outside the building. To cut costs, the company's accounting department had suggested less frequent use of central air conditioning and had instructed employees to open their windows to create circulation in the two floors that PCI occupied in its Phoenix location. It was therefore no surprise that the loud sound of the highway matched the loud back-and-forth arguments between the two men in the room, and that very little could be overheard or understood; no one knew what would emerge from the heated discussion. What was certain, however was that a great deal of tension was in the warm Phoenix air that had crept through the windows.

THE BUSINESS MODEL OF PHOENIX CARDS INC.

Phoenix Cards Inc. (PCI) was one of the first suppliers of gift cards in the US market, supplying thousands of retail outlets such as supermarkets, gift shops, and discount stores with a range of gift cards and prepaid debit cards. The company was launched in 1991 when gift cards began to be widely adopted by the general population and as the use of cash for purposes of gift-giving became less popular. PCI was eventually sold by the two founding brothers to a national bank, which had acquired PCI in its desire to diversify its banking operations following deregulation of the banking industry in the US. PCI first distributed its cards in the states of Arizona, California and Nevada. The company expanded distribution nationally in the 2000s.

Gift cards and prepaid debit cards are sold by many retailers. These cards provide buyers with the ability to gift money to friends, family and colleagues and at the same time provide the recipient with the flexibility to shop for whatever they need or desire. In the early days of the existence of these cards, the public view on their use was mixed. Some consumer advocates claimed that the cards removed the burden of finding the right gift from the person purchasing the card to the recipient, while critics believed that this made the gift giving process less personal and could convey a reduced degree of engagement between the gift giver and the recipient of the gift. Despite such criticisms and initial consumer resistance, public use of gift cards and prepaid debit cards grew dramatically over the years. As a result, it was estimated that about 60% of the population purchases or receives prepaid debit cards or gift cards in any one year time period.

The cards that PCI sold would typically be displayed immediately next to the cash register in the retail outlet. In some cases the cards would be integrated with the existing store display at the point-of-sale (POS) immediately next to the cash register, and in other cases, the cards would be displayed on a stand-alone display supplied by PCI to each retailer. Placement of the gift card displays near the cash register was the industry norm and it was believed by most industry professionals that the immediate access to the cashier would speed up the activation of the card, encourage purchases of the cards, and in some cases also encourage impulse buying behavior by customers who may have not considered purchasing gift cards prior to entering the retail outlet.

PCI's featured cards were from 14 major retail chains and 4 major credit card brands. These cards were supplied in denominations of $10, $50 and $100. Hawking believed that given the rate of inflation and growth in consumer spending at times of gift giving, PCI should begin to move up in the denominations sold, and also provide $250 and $500 cards. To his knowledge only three other competitors had such offerings, and such an offering would help improve PCI's competitiveness in the marketplace. However, to effectively market such unique offerings to retailers, a strong sales effort backed by a trained and motivated sales force would be needed.

MARKET RESEARCH ON GIFT CARDS AND PREPAID DEBIT CARDS

PCI had recently commissioned two market research studies involving both focus groups and surveys to understand the marketplace in which it competes. The first study focused on individuals who regularly purchase gift cards and was intended to uncover the thought process that guides their decision to buy a gift card. The three focus groups conducted for this study utilized samples of retail shoppers who had recently (past 90 days) purchased a gift card, and showed the following factors (in descending order of importance) that influence their decision: (1) Brand name and/or reputation of the retailer associated with the gift card; (2) The close proximity of the gift card display to the cashier (3) The graphics shown on the card. The second study focused on the retailers who decide to feature an in-store display of gift cards and/or debit cards. This study used a national survey and found the following three factors (in descending order of importance) to affect the decision making of retail managers: (1) Personal experience working with the salesperson selling the cards; (2)

The assistance of the sales person in maintaining and restocking the gift card display; (3) The reputation of the company supplying the gift cards.

Hawking had asked one of his assistants to supplement the research summarized below with a simple calendared tabulation of PCI's card sales (in terms of the number of cards sold) for the past 3 years. The resulting chart is shown above. Hawking's personal forecast suggested that PCI sales were not only healthy but likely to double in the next three years. His observation stemmed from the fact that PCI's card sales had grown steadily every year, and he saw no reason for this growth to be challenged in the coming years. Industry trends showed similar growth rates over the past years.

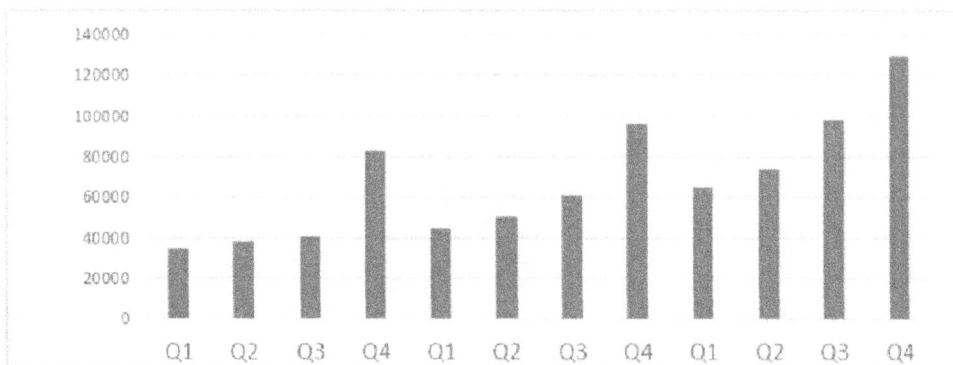

PCI'S DISTRIBUTION MODEL

PCI sold its cards through a representative system and did not have its own sales force. Unified Sales Operations (USO) was the company that provided PCI with the representatives. USO representatives supplied retailers around the country with a range of products and services, and PCI's products were among the inventory of items they offered to the thousands of retail outlets they served. USO had worked with PCI for the past 15 years and the partnership had, for the most part, worked well. USO's representatives would visit the stores, stock inventory of cards, ensure that PCI's card displays are prominently located and well maintained. In addition to maintaining the inventory of gift cards on display at the PCI card stands, the USO representative also supplied the retail outlet with other items that USO had been commissioned to sell from other manufacturers and suppliers.

The USO reps were not paid a fixed salary for their work and were paid on commission basis only. For every card they sold, USO would receive a 5% commission, half of which would be given to the representative. Although the commission payment agreement with USO was lower than the typical industry norm of 7.5%, the commitment that USO had to take on was limited as neither USO nor its representatives had to invest in terms of taking on ownership of the inventory of PCI cards that they had to sell. The typical USO sales rep could visit 6 retailers each day, and the typical retailer required one visit every 6 weeks to help retain the business. Any cards the USO reps were not able to sell could be returned to PCI through an inventory recovery agreement between PCI and USO. In addition to PCI's cards, USO reps also sold other products to the retailers they visited, including flash lights, cigarette lighters, products featured on infomercials, and select dietary supplements. Most of these products would be displayed in the point-of-sale display area near the cash registers, and as a result a common source of contention between USO and companies that commissioned it to distribute their products was which products were given the priority and more prominently displayed.

Store Size (square ft.)	Number of retail outlets that USO serves	Number of retail outlets nationally that are in this size category	Average Annual Profit Margin for PCI for Each Store
Less than 2,000	18,155	925,914	$1,891
2,000-5,000	941	44,375	$2,350
5,000-10,000	389	24,805	$4,109
Over 10,000	185	21,129	$12,362

USO's representatives reached a total of 19,670 retail outlets throughout the United States. The table above shows the distribution of USO's activities across the different retail store size categories. Hawking believed that while USO has been effective in reaching a large number of retail outlets, its representation in the marketplace is below where it should be. For example, in his view, USO's representation in large stores, such as major retail chains and department stores, was weak. Hawking believed that the low penetration in the larger stores inhibited PCI's long-term growth. In his view, the unwillingness of USO to push PCI's cards to the larger stores was a stumbling block that could only be addressed if a total overhaul of the sales process is done. This was one of his main objectives behind his request to hire 34 sales people – the main point of contention with Xavier.

In addition to his frustration with having very little representation in larger stores, Hawking was quite upset that USO had not helped promote some of the new lines of products that PCI had introduced. Specifically, earlier in the year, PCI had introduced travel insurance and dental discount cards – both of which could be purchased in the form of cards on the displays featuring PCI's gift cards and prepaid debit cards. USO representatives had resisted promoting these new products to some of the retailers, for fear that these new products would take shelf space away from the current inventory of gift cards and prepaid debit cards that the PCI displays hold and hence hinder representatives' commission income. The USO representatives also questioned if the selling of travel insurance and dental discount cards is something that would be acceptable to consumers, most of whom had never purchased such products through store displays of any type.

Despite having been available for over 6 months, the supplemental dental discount cards and travel insurance plans offered by PCI had hardly achieved any acceptable foothold in retail outlets. As of June, only 231 travel policy cards and 35 dental discount cards were sold nationally. Yet, from a profit margin perspective, these two new products presented PCI with margins that were nearly triple the average margin for PCIs gift cards and debit cards. The inability to tap into this opportunity was a source of increasing frustration for Hawking. To remedy the frustrations arriving from the current situation, Hawking had proposed to the hiring of a dedicated sales force. The sales force he envisioned would take full ownership for reaching out to the retail outlets that USO was serving. The sales force would also go beyond these existing retail outlets, which had prior experience using PCI's displays, and extend to the retail outlets that USO had not secured representation in. Hawking estimated that the cost of each sales person (both salaries, travel and bonuses) would be $89,500 annually. In addition, given that the sales context for PCI's products was unique, about $10,000 in training costs would be needed. Furthermore, the typical recruited sales person would not be expected to generate much sales for the first three months of being on the sales force. In addition to the 34 sales people that Hawking had proposed, a sales manager working out of PCI's head office would be hired, at an annual cost of $180,000 (salary, benefits, and commissions).

CASE QUESTION

Do you agree with Hawking or Xavier, and why?

HOME ENDORSERS INC.

Home Endorsers Inc. (HEI) is a small mortgage broker located in Wayne, NY. HEI was established in the early 1990s by Janet McIntyre and George Mavis, two business school graduates from a private university in upstate New York. After its inception, the company gradually grew in both mortgage volume and client base. HEI witnessed considerable growth because of the housing boom cycles and growing consumer interest in purchasing real estate properties. HEI had multiple branches in other cities in New York State and considered plans for expanding beyond state lines.

HEI often had repeat customers, and positive customer experience created considerable word-of-mouth advertising for the company; friends and relatives of many previous homebuyers applied for their mortgages through HEI. Despite contentment with their own success and the notable growth of HEI's mortgage volume, McIntyre and Mavis decided to objectively examine the company's performance by carefully studying some of their competitors in local markets. A market research firm was hired to document the mortgage origination volume of HEI's competitors and to compare and contrast their business practices with those of HEI.

The market research report, which was delivered to McIntyre and Mavis, caused considerable alarm. The numbers suggested that HEI was performing at considerably lower levels than its competition. For example, the mortgage origination volume of these competitors and that of HEI differed noticeably. In the previous four years, the mortgage origination volume of HEI had grown by 78%. While this number may seem impressive at first glance, it was disappointing when compared to some of its direct competitors who, on average, experienced a 115% growth rate. Furthermore, the market research firm, through an examination of the mortgage records filed at local government offices, estimated that the competitors' revenues from administrative fees and additional charges was at least twice that of HEI.

Mavis and McIntyre were alarmed by these numbers because they hinted at the possibility that HEI was leaving considerable amounts of profit on the table and was not realizing all revenue potential in its dealings with homebuyers. In fact, the financial burdens of growth and the costs of establishing new branch offices required them to find additional sources of revenue. They asked the market research firm to examine further the activities of some of the competing mortgage brokers. The consulting team decided to utilize two specific sources of data. The first source was focus groups conducted with recent homebuyers who had purchased their homes with mortgages supplied by these competitors. These individuals could be easily identified through property records and mortgage documents made publicly available at local government offices. The second source of data was consumer complaint records filed with regulatory bodies and consumer protection agencies, which might provide insights on the business practices of some of these competitors.

FOCUS GROUPS

Three focus group sessions were held with recent homebuyers who had used the mortgage products of some of HEI's competitors. The focus groups were designed to help the researchers understand the mortgage selection process of homebuyers and the application procedures of competitors. These groups also helped identify good and bad business practices used by the competing mortgage brokers.

Each focus group was comprised of six to ten individuals, and the conversations were recorded and transcribed for subsequent analysis.

The results indicated that homebuyers in general do not have a great deal of knowledge about the various companies and mortgage brokers in their local areas. Most could only name three other mortgage brokers that they were aware of, or had come into contact with, in their neighborhoods. Their choice of a mortgage company was often affected by recommendations made by the real estate agent. Focus group participants also indicated that they were often attracted to a particular broker through advertising in print or on cable TV in which low interest rates were mentioned. One-on-one contact with the mortgage broker and the personal attention given to the mortgage applicant were also considered important in their decisions.

Several focus group participants mentioned that, while the low advertised mortgage rates were the primary attraction, they were surprised at the hidden fees and 'closing costs' that appeared last-minute at the time of closing the contract. The homebuyers believed they were not made fully aware of the fees ahead of time, but could not dispute them since they were informed within a very short time—typically two days or less—of the purchase date of the house. Disputing these charges would require delaying the closing date or the termination of the purchase contract, which is often associated with stiff penalties such as the loss of the down-payment made on the property.

CONSUMER COMPLAINT RECORDS

The consulting team also examined public information related to the selected companies that was made available through consumer protection agencies, local government offices, and court documents. A series of questionable business practices were revealed through such analysis. In particular, homebuyers frequently experienced the following cases when interacting with these mortgage companies:

Bait-and-Switch: Mortgages advertised with attractive interest rates. Without disclosing such information in the ad, the rate only applied to applicants with unusually high credit scores. Most homebuyers who proceeded to contact the broker found upon the completion of their mortgage application that the interest rate they would be charged exceeded the advertised rate.

Step-Up-Pricing: Mortgage applicants were faced with last-minute fees that they were not clearly informed about until shortly before the closing date. Often, this resulted in the payment of thousands of dollars of additional fees by the homebuyer. Homebuyers rarely disputed these fees due to the time constraints placed on them and the financial penalties of backing out from the purchase of the property.

Affiliated-Providers: Mortgage companies explicitly or implicitly required the homebuyer to obtain homeowners insurance from affiliated insurance companies or to conduct the property inspection from a list of pre-approved inspectors. The rates charged by some of these affiliates were found to be higher than prevailing market rates. Furthermore, in certain cases, a commission structure was in place to compensate the mortgage company for channeling business to the affiliates.

These practices were found to take place across different residential markets, ranging from small apartments to luxury homes. They were often associated with the mortgage brokers being charged fines for violating specific regulations. However, these punitive measures only occurred in the rare cases in which homebuyers made the effort to report the case or pursued legal action against the mortgage company. In the majority of cases, homebuyers seemed to move on with their lives without legally confronting their mortgage providers, leaving few, if any, public records of their experience.

DECISION FACING MCINTYRE AND MAVIS

HEI's future, as well as its ability to maintain its financial health and to grow, largely depended on the ability of Mavis and McIntyre to find new sources of income. Given the questionable approaches used by their competitors to boost their own revenue streams, the two former college classmates were faced with ethical dilemmas which they never had to confront as college students.

CASE QUESTIONS

1. What ethical issues do you find relevant to the practices of HEI's competitors?

2. How should McIntyre and Mavis respond to these practices?

3. What examples of marketing practices similar to those used by HEI's competitors have you seen profiled in the press?

PIONEER ACCELERATED MORTGAGE

On a Wednesday afternoon in late October, Hillary Walters received a surprising phone call from one of the leading consumer protection agencies in the state of Maryland. Walters, the Marketing Vice President for Pioneer Accelerated Mortgage Inc. (PAM), was informed of a number of consumer complaints filed by individuals who had applied for mortgages through the company's web site. A total of eight complainants had accused PAM of misleading advertising practices. They claimed the company stated in its Internet banner ads that their customers' mortgage applications would be processed and approved in less than 24 hours. In all eight cases, the applicants were emailed a "preliminary approval" within hours of filing their applications. However, within two days, they had all been contacted by PAM and informed that their mortgage application was subsequently denied. Walters was told that the agency might pursue a class action law suit against PAM on the grounds of deceptive advertising and that federal and state regulators would also be informed.

PAM'S MARKETING STRATEGY

Pioneer Accelerated Mortgage Inc. was an online mortgage provider based in Bethesda, Maryland. The company was established in the late 1990s as a broker of mortgage products and subsequently became the primary issuer of mortgages. Most of PAM's business was conducted online and, with the growth of the Internet and the boom in the real estate market, the company experienced significant growth in its mortgage volume. At the time of the case study, PAM employed 46 individuals across a variety of marketing, legal, administrative, and sales functions.

PAM's primary customer acquisition strategy capitalized on intense banner advertising on the Internet. In addition, the company established partnerships with real estate search web sites and online credit search engines. Once a homebuyer clicked through PAM's links, the application process was completed online. The banner ads and Internet links promoted the company's quick application processing and competitive mortgage rates. The ads also emphasized its commitment to a 24-hour turnaround time on mortgage application decisions, which was guaranteed by a $200 deduction in closing fees in case this failed to occur. The aggressive positioning of the company seemed to create considerable consumer interest and, as a result, the click-through rates for PAM's Internet ads were considerably higher than the average for the industry.

THE APPLICATION PROCESS

The mortgage application process at PAM had five stages. The first stage consisted of collecting background information on the homebuyer through the PAM web site. The collected information included items such as the individual's name, social security number, date of birth, place of employment, annual income, existing assets, and other relevant personal and financial information. Once this information was collected, the second stage of application processing was conducted by using the applicant's personal information to access credit records and to obtain the individual's credit score. This information, along with data on the property being purchased, was then used to arrive at the "preliminary decision." The third stage of the application process consisted of informing the applicant of the preliminary decision, usually via email. PAM had a 24-hour turnaround commitment to mortgage applicants for completing Stage Three of the process. The fourth stage of the application process consisted of conducting detailed background research on each application. For example, verification of the place of employment, income validation, and criminal background checks were conducted during this stage. Stage Four often took between one and three days to complete. The final stage of the process consisted of confirming application approval or denial decisions. Applicants for whom insufficient or unfavorable background information was revealed in Stage Four were sent out a "denial of mortgage application" (DMA) email. Those whose mortgage application had been approved were sent confirmation emails and were requested to initiate the processing of legal paperwork, if applicable. The exhibit below is a flowchart of the application processing procedures used by PAM.

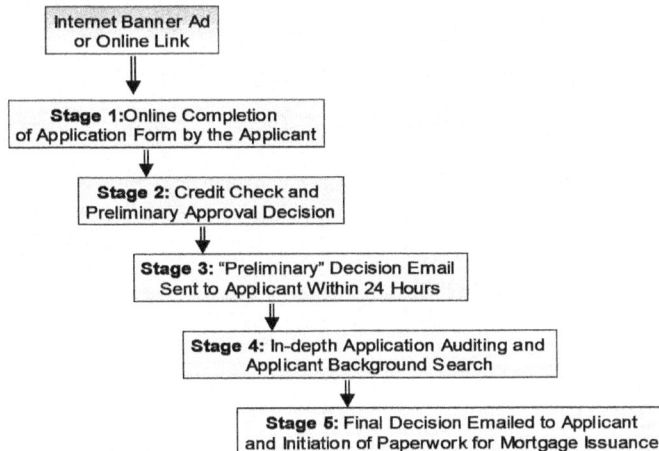

Despite the streamlined approach to application processing, the entire process was a costly and, at times, labor-intensive activity. For example, in order to attract applicants through banner advertising, a large number of Internet impressions were needed. It was estimated that the banner advertising cost associated with a single applicant's click-through to the application page (Stage One) was about $38. Conducting the required credit checks and communicating the decision to the applicant via email (Stages Two and Three) was estimated to cost $26. Stages Four and Five, which required more labor-intensive activities, detailed decision-making, and often resulted in one-on-one phone conversations between applicants and customer service staff, cost PAM approximately $85 per application. This brought the total cost of processing a single completed application to well over $100.

To better understand the claims made against PAM by the consumer protection agency, Walters asked one of her mangers to obtain data related to the company's mortgage applications for the first half of the current calendar year. In particular, data on the number of mortgages that completed Stages Three and Five of the process were needed. Walters also wanted to examine the applicant pool in more detail by separately studying the numbers for different mortgage amounts. The exhibit below provides a summary of the findings from the applications filed.

	Mortgage Amount Under $100,000	Mortgage Amount $100,000-$249,999	Mortgage Amount $250,000-499,999	Mortgage Amount $500,000 and higher
Number of Applications	83	138	110	78
Number Approved Same Day (Stage 3)	61	103	84	53
Number Denied in Stage 5	7	4	4	8

While the application statistics shown in the exhibit indicated a significant number of Stage Five application rejections, Walters was unclear of the reason why the numbers were so high. Stage Five rejections were the primary source of consumer complaints, and understanding their nature was essential to developing an educated strategy in response to the crisis. Discussion with the administrative staff and subsequent analysis revealed that, in nearly every case, the applicants who were denied had provided inaccurate or misleading information on their background. For example, an applicant may have reported an income level higher than their true earnings, over-stated their assets or understated their existing credit obligations. In some cases, individuals listed as references in the application were contacted by phone and provided inconsistent or unfavorable information about the applicant. This was good news for Walters because it suggested that Stage Five application rejections could most likely be defended based on applicants' misrepresentation of personal information. While this was reassuring to Walters, the numbers revealed in this exercise prompted her and other senior management at PAM to question the company's overall promotional policies. The numbers implied a lack of a segment-based approach to marketing the company's products as well as the need for a better understanding of applicants' thought processes.

MARKET RESEARCH

To answer some of these emerging questions, Walters commissioned Hanzen Intelligence and Research Enterprise (HIRE) to conduct a survey of recent mortgage applicants. The study's primary objective was to reveal the rate of applicant misinformation and some of the factors contributing to application inaccuracies among PAM mortgage applicants. While the subject of this line of questioning was PAM's current applicant pool, company policy restricted surveying this group for regulatory reasons. As a result, it was necessary to conduct primary market research using a sample of the population to arrive at estimates of overall misinformation rates and related attitudinal measures. HIRE's access to a large market research panel of Internet users was a valuable asset because most of PAM's applicants were also Internet users. An analysis of HIRE panel member demographics revealed similarities with PAM's applicant pool, making the group relevant for a market survey.

Emails were sent out by HIRE to its panel members who had recently reported purchasing a residential property. A total of 1,287 panel members who had purchased a home in the past twelve months were contacted, and 318 individuals responded to the survey. Each panel member was given a monetary incentive and the opportunity to win small home electronics products through a lottery. The survey consisted of 38 questions administered through an Internet questionnaire distribution web site. Respondents were asked an array of questions related to their finances, including their perceptions of mortgage companies and information needs when applying for mortgages. In order to prevent bias in the responses of participants, eighteen of the 38 questions used were unrelated to mortgages. However, two specific mortgage-related questions were of particular interest to Walters: "Mortgage companies request excessive amounts of unnecessary personal information", and "Mortgage companies do not have the right to ask for too much personal information." Respondents were asked to respond either "yes" or "no" to these two questions. In addition, the questionnaire asked respondents to state their total mortgage amount for their recent home purchase. The exhibit below summarizes the results.

	Mortgage Amount Under $100,000	Mortgage Amount $100,000-$249,999	Mortgage Amount $250,000-$499,999	Mortgage Amount $500,000 and higher
Number of Respondents	95	143	48	32
Number Agreeing with the statement … *"Mortgage companies request excessive amounts of unnecessary personal information"*	52	55	17	19
Number Agreeing with the statement … *"Mortgage companies do not have the right to ask for too much personal information"*	40	59	18	24

CASE QUESTIONS

1. How should PAM adjust its marketing programs in order to focus its promotions on specific segments of the market?

2. Based on the survey research, what is your estimate of the percentage of PAM's mortgage applicants who believe that mortgage companies require excessive amounts of personal information?

AUTHOR'S BIOGRAPHY

Hooman Estelami is a professor of marketing at the Gabelli School of Business, Fordham University in New York. He received his Ph.D. in marketing from Columbia University and his MBA from McGill University. His areas of specialization are financial services marketing, pricing, customer service management, and distance education. He has received multiple awards for his teaching and research and has advised a wide range of corporations on target marketing, pricing, and service enhancement strategies.

In addition to this book, he is the author of five other books: *Marketing Financial Services; Marketing Turnarounds; The Routledge Companion to Financial Services Marketing; Predictors of Victory and Injury in Mixed Martial Arts Combat;* and *Frontiers of Distance Learning in Business Education.*

His research has appeared in a wide range of journals including: *International Journal of Research in Marketing, Journal of the Academy of Marketing Science, Journal of Business Research, Journal of Consumer Affairs, Journal of Financial Services Marketing, Journal of Retailing, Journal of Service Research, Journal of Product and Brand Management, Journal of Consumer Behaviour, Journal of Promotion Management, Journal of Marketing Education, American Journal of Business Education,* and *Marketing Education Review.*

He is the editor of the *International Journal of Bank Marketing*, and previously served as the associate editor of the *Journal of Product and Brand Management.*

www.ingramcontent.com/pod-product-compliance
Lightning Source LLC
Chambersburg PA
CBHW051224200326
41519CB00025B/7236